The Donigers of Great Neck

D^{The}onigers

of GREAT NECK

A MYTHOLOGIZED MEMOIR

Wendy Doniger

Brandeis University Press
Waltham, Massachusetts

BRANDEIS UNIVERSITY PRESS

An imprint of University Press of New England

www.upne.com

© 2019 Wendy Doniger

All rights reserved

Manufactured in the United States of America

Designed by Eric M. Brooks

Typeset in Arno Pro by Passumpsic Publishing

Front cover images: Lester Doniger and his sister Sonja in
Raczki, circa 1920. Rita Doniger as a little girl in Vienna, in
front of the Hofburg, with an unknown woman.

Library of Congress Cataloging-in-Publication Data
available upon request

Hardcover ISBN: 978-1-5126-0351-4

Paperback ISBN: 978-1-5126-0352-1

Ebook ISBN: 978-1-5126-0353-8

5 4 3 2 1

CONTENTS

ACKNOWLEDGMENTS

I never could have written this book at all had I
not had the help of members of my family and my old
friends in dredging up and comparing and correcting our
shared memories. They remembered *so much* that I had
forgotten. I am particularly grateful to my brothers Jerry
and Tony, their wives Kay and Liza, Lucy Lunt, and my
son Mike, who not only talked with me for hours and
hours, correcting and adding and suggesting, but also
read several early drafts of the book, again correcting
and adding and suggesting. Julia Kahn (Shubik), Cecily
Orenstein (Morse), and Isabeth Rosenberg (Gross)
talked me through many hazy memories of our shared
youth in Great Neck. My oldest friend, Cynthia Norris
(Graae), not only supplied me with her own fascinating
insights into my earliest years but read a draft of the
book and made numerous editorial corrections, always
clarifying and tightening and sharpening my writing.
Annie Dillard set an inspiring example with her own
magnificent memoir of her parents, *An American
Childhood*, and usefully kept warning me against Mommy
Dearest. And Lorraine Daston read an early draft and
responded with enthusiasm and insights that nourished
and inspired me through all subsequent revisions. To all
of them, I dedicate this book.

TIMELINE

1909	Lester is born
1911	Rita is born
1920	Lester comes to America
1931	Lester graduates from NYU
1931	Jerry is born
1940	Wendy is born
1950	Tony is born
1958–62	Wendy attends Radcliffe
1960	Wendy marries Mr. Wrong (1962 divorces him)
1963–64	Wendy goes to India
1963	Rita visits Wendy in India
1964	Wendy marries again (1980 divorces him)
1965–75	Wendy is in Oxford
1968–75	Wendy is lecturer at the School of Oriental and African Studies in London
1970–71	Wendy is in Moscow
1971	April 27: Lester dies
	November 5: Michael is born
1975–78	Wendy teaches in Berkeley
1978–2019	Wendy teaches at the University of Chicago
1991	August 8: Rita dies

Many Memories, Many Myths

I can remember a little girl. . . . Where is she now? Yes,
"Where are the snows of yesteryear?" . . . But how can it
really be, that I was the little girl, the little Resi, and that I will
also someday be the old woman — the old woman, the old
Marschallin. "Look, there she goes, the old princess Resi!"
But how can that happen? How does God do it? When I am
still always the same.

> *Der Rosenkavalier*, Act 1, lyrics by
> Hugo von Hofmannsthal[1]

The project of retrieving my memories of my parents, Lester and Rita Doniger, to put into a book began when the American Council of Learned Societies invited me to give, in May of 2015, the Charles Haskins Prize Lecture, which was supposed to be about my "life of learning." (You can see my Haskins Lecture online at www.acls.org. From time to time, I have found it unavoidable to recycle bits of the Haskins Lecture in this book for essential pieces of the plot.) I wrote about the people from whom I had learned, and as I wrote, my mother loomed larger and larger, and I fully realized for the first time how much I owed her.

And so, when I was invited to give the Mandel Lectures at Brandeis, in that autumn of 2015, and to use, if I wished, an "unconventional format," I decided to take this opportunity to write about my parents.

I tried to stick to the Jack Webb approach: nothing but the facts, ma'am.* But the deeper, Freudian, Proustian level kept bubbling up. I had started from the present, the point of view of an aging academic, but then the child's view kept breaking into the adult's story. In the end, there turned out to be several significantly different visions of many events. In the historical prequel (Chapter 1), a lot of fairly hazy mythology, consisting primarily of stories I had heard about who each of my parents was before they met. In the two early histories of my parents (Chapters 2 and 3), more factual material, some verified by the records. (Where there are such verifiable sources, I've noted them in endnotes.) For the years when I knew them (Chapter 4), still some episodes that could be corroborated, but now heavily colored by my subjective evaluation of them. And when it came to writing about my own relationship with each of my parents (Chapter 5), during the thirty (or fifty) years I knew my father and my mother (respectively), and the forty-five (or twenty-five) years I have lived without them, I found myself drowning in several different subjectivities, some

*For those who do not remember the 1950s, Jack Webb was the star of *Dragnet*; he played a cop who kept trying to keep people from giving their opinions of things, by insisting, "Nothing but the facts, ma'am."

dredged up from the past and others just breaking into my awareness now. I tried, with middling success, to keep myself out of the story, lurking in the wings until Chapter 5, when I allow myself to join my parents on center stage. But since I could not help referring to myself from time to time, I have supplied a timeline (xi) giving the main events of their lives as they intersected with mine.

Inevitably, my story exists along a continuum from the factual to the mythological. As a woman who has worked on mythological texts for half a century,[2] I know a myth when I see one, and I see this memoir as heavily mythologized. Through a kind of occupational handicap, I remember best the things that make the best stories, and I have trouble resisting the impulse to make them into better stories. But this is a heightened version of what we all do. For we do not remember the past; we remember our memories of the past, the stories we've told ourselves about the past, and the stories that others have told us. Memory is a chameleon; it changes into the person it's talking to, like Woody Allen's Zelig (in *Zelig*, 1983), and accommodates itself to our present needs. Freud taught us that we never remember the dream, only the secondary revision that we tell ourselves as we wake. And so it is with personal histories.

We can wake up briefly at points in this dream: there are birth certificates, passports, photographs with dates scribbled on the back. I have newspaper clippings about Lester that supply a few reliable dates. And for Rita, I actually have two archives of her own words. One is the collection of her notes (Appendix 2), and the other is a tape recording made for an NPR program about me that Adam Phillips did in 1990. Because NPR still had generous budgets in those golden days, Phillips flew with me to Great Neck and interviewed Rita, too. He used only a few minutes of Rita's words in the final cut, but I still have the full hour's recording, from which I have cited several astonishingly frank statements that she made. Here, you might think, is the brutal truth, reality. And yet, and yet, 1990 was near the end of Rita's life, when she wasn't always quite in her right mind, and I wonder, when she spoke of the past, just how accurately her words at that time represented the reality of the way she had felt about the events when they had happened so long ago. Mythmaking was at work here, too.

There also are moments when we intersect with other peoples' versions of our past history. I have two brothers, one ten years older than me (Jerry) and one ten years younger (Tony), and any time I tell a part of my story about our parents to either of them, he's almost certain to say, "No, it wasn't like that; it was like this." (And since one of my brothers is a lawyer, he's probably right.)[3] But I can only tell you my version, my mythologized memory, which is all I really have. The version that matters to me, the one that I carry within me, defies all other versions of the events. As Oliver Sacks has said of Freud's view of memory, we "retranscribe" our remembrances over and over again, so that, even when we are in the grip of false memories or inadvertent plagiarism, "Our only truth is narrative truth, the stories we tell each other and ourselves — the stories we continually recategorize and refine."[4] And this process of retranscribing (*Nachträglichkeit*) is one of the most basic sources of our creativity.

One problem I encountered from the start was a matter of balance. Where Lester was intense but quiet, Rita was more dramatic and eclectic, not to say wildly idiosyncratic. Lester was a man of discreet virtue who did not wear his heart on his sleeve; he smoldered rather than exploded, and found subtle ways to manage Rita without generating an actual fight. She, by contrast, was far more aggressive (or at least passive-aggressive) in devising ways to express her suppressed fury about many aspects of her life, including her marriage. So he inspired far fewer anecdotes than she did. This imbalance was further compounded by the fact that she lived twenty years longer than he did, generating two more decades of material. I tried to rectify the balance, but she still dominates the book.

In any case, I can tell you only a fraction of my parents' lives, the portion that is part of who I am. But I hope that this fragment will leave you with an idea of what it was like for me to come to know my parents' stories, and how those stories became part of my own story, and how their stories kept changing as I looked back on them from the steadily widening distance between their deaths and my ongoing life.

I can at least tell their still-evolving stories as truthfully as possible. Ian Parker, writing about the books that Edward St. Aubyn wrote about his ghastly childhood, remarked, "Even if St. Aubyn's memories of his earlier life, shaped by trauma, are not perfectly accurate, he seems to take care to transmit his memories accurately." And he quotes St. Aubyn as saying, of those books, "The truth for me is the truth in the books. . . . And the truth in the facts is a derelict ruin."[5] For my story, it's not that I've made up memories; it's that my memory has made up those memories. But those stories have a truth of their own, and I can be true to that truth. Even if none of it had happened, all of it would be true to the life I lived, because I always believed it.

Hugo von Hofmannsthal's lyrics for the Marschallin's soliloquy from the first act of Richard Strauss's *Der Rosenkavalier*, my mother's favorite opera and mine too, cited at the opening of this prelude, are a fitting motto for this memoir. My parents were many different people, and I knew only a few of them. Nor did they live to meet all of the many people I was to become. But this is my story of the lives that we shared.

CHAPTER ONE

My Parents' Childhoods in Europe (and America)

A red thread runs through my story, and I do mean *red*, for Russia played a role in all three of our lives: Lester was born in Russia; Rita was devoted to Stalin and died in the week when the Soviet Union began to fall; and during the year that I lived in Moscow, Lester died and I conceived my son. So let us begin in Russia at the dawn of World War I.

Lester's Childhood in Raczki...

Almost all that I know of my father's childhood I owe to the earaches that plagued me in my own childhood. The only thing that seemed to cure them was having my mother heat some olive oil in a big spoon over the kitchen stove's flame, and then pour the oil into my ear and stop it up with a ball of cotton. But that was just the first half of the treatment; the second half was to have my father sit beside me as I lay on the couch on my side, and tell me stories of his childhood.

Eleazar (Lazar, called Leshki) Doniger (who became Lester Lawrence Doniger at Ellis Island) was born in 1909. His birthday was said to be October 15, but there were no public records for Jews in those days, and he made the date up. (His brother Jack chose January 1 so that he would be sure to remember it.) Lester was born to Moses Doniger (born in 1868) and Celia Mira Jakut Doniger (born c. 1870) in Raczki, a town that was eleven miles from the market town of Suvalki, which was near the port city of Königsberg, a.k.a. Kaliningrad (one hundred thirty miles from Raczki). Raczki then belonged to Russia but was near Poland (and now is *in* Poland), and also near (or sometimes *in*) Germany. Lester was the youngest of five children; his older brother, Jack (born in 1890), was twenty years older than Lester; then came Simon (1896), Sonja (1903), Katy (c. 1906), and Lester (1909). (I've called this book *The Donigers of Great Neck*, meaning my parents and siblings and myself, but really we were part of a larger network of Great Neck Donigers, including the families of my father's brothers Jack and Simon, who play only a minor part in my story. See the genealogy, 153).

They spoke Yiddish at home and Russian, rather than Polish, at school. Lester never forgot his Yiddish. Often, when he felt that someone was taking too seriously a matter that Lester regarded as relatively minor, he remarked, "Alle yidden . . . ," the first words of a well-known Yiddish saying that can be translated, "All the Jews should have such problems." He also remembered a lot of his Russian, and used to sing a Russian lullaby to me that that began, "Spi mladenets, moi prekrasni," and always sounded to me like, "See my dentist, more Bing Crosby." (Years later, when I lived in Moscow, I learned that the words were actually written by the poet Lermontov and meant, "Sleep, my baby, my pretty one.") Lester had random Russian habits, like drinking his tea "po-Russki," which is to say, taking a lump of sugar in his teeth and drinking his tea through it. I have two photographs of Lester as a little boy in Russia (Figures 2 and 3).

A bit of family mythology suggests that Lester was begotten (when his mother was forty) not by Moses Doniger, but by the German schoolteacher in the town. Aside from possible DNA interest, that this story, true or false, could be told at all is evidence of the intimacy between the Jews and the Germans in Raczki, an intimacy that is at the heart of an important incident in Lester's early life. It seems that in around 1915, when he was six years old, Lester was playing with his friends on one of those small handcars or pump trolleys that were used on railroad tracks in those days. He fell off, and the car ran over his leg, crushing it badly. Since none of the Russian (or Polish) doctors in the town would set the leg of a Jew, Lester would probably have died of gangrene. But this was World War I, and a German garrison had broken through the Russian lines and occupied the town. A German doctor saved Lester's leg and his life.

Lester told me this story when I was five or six years old, in 1945 or '46, lying on the couch with the cotton in my ear. World War II had just ended. If ever there was a war in which we knew who were the good guys and who the bad guys, that was the war. We all knew that the Germans had tried to annihilate the Jews, and in our household, at least, we knew that the Russians in general, and Stalin in particular, had won the war and thus delivered the Jews from the fiery furnace. How, then, I asked my father, was it possible that a *German* doctor had saved his life? Oh, said he, of course the Poles and Russians were much worse antisemites than the Germans.

My young brain could not process this new information. The Germans were the good guys, the Russians the bad guys? My basic ethical cosmology was shattered forever. And indeed, I date from that moment my deep-seated distrust of any generalization about the moral worth of any group, or indeed any confident assertion of the moral distribution in any political conflict. I never again thought that I really knew who were the good guys and who the bad guys.

I learned more about antisemitism from the stories Lester told about the Polish and Russian children in Raczki, stories about incidents that revealed antipathy but never violence. In one of his anecdotes, the Jewish boys had gone to bathe in the village swimming hole and left their clothes on the bank; the Polish/Russian boys stole their clothes, and Lester and his friends had to wait until it was dark to walk home through the town naked.[6] There were no pogroms in any of Lester's stories.

... and America

The aftermath of the story of Lester's broken leg also became part of Doniger family mythology. Most of his immediate family left Russia in 1920, during the Russian Civil War. (Jack and Simon had come over to America earlier, and Simon then went back to bring the rest of them out, together: the three remaining children — Lester and his two sisters — and both parents.[7]) According to the received history (received by me, at least), Lester's leg still slowed him down (it was always a bit crooked), and his older sister Katy carried him most of the way. I had always imagined them walking hundreds of miles, carrying their belongings in bundles wrapped in cloth on the end of poles slung over their shoulders, like comic strip hobos or characters in *Fiddler on the Roof*. But once I learned a bit of geography, I realized that they had left by boat, via the Baltic seaport of Königsberg/Kaliningrad. Still, Katy might have carried Lester the hundred and twenty-five miles to the port. In any case, she died in America in 1939, of a weak heart. Here again, the family mythologizing machine kicks in: I always thought her heart was damaged carrying Lester out of Russia, but her son, Jerry, always thought her heart was damaged giving birth to him, in 1931. In any case, in 1938, while Katy was dying, much too young (only thirty-two or so), her husband sent Jerry, just seven years old, to visit my parents and never returned for him. Lester and Rita adopted him. I was born a few years later and inherited him as my older (ten-year-old) brother. But I am getting ahead of my story.

I remember Lester's parents as very old people who smelled funny. Moses Doniger died in 1946, when I was five and he was seventy-eight, and Celia died within months of him. They seemed, even to a child like me, very small.

When Lester's family came to America, at first they all lived in Brooklyn, at 1221 Lincoln Place. In 1926, when Lester was seventeen years old and a senior at Boys' High, Brooklyn, he entered an oratorical contest sponsored by New York University. Speaking on "The Problems of Armament," he won first prize, $250 to be used as a scholarship anywhere in the country.[8] Contestants had to speak for half an hour on a topic that was announced only the night before, but the general scope of the topic was known in advance. Lester wrote a twenty-minute speech on the general topic, and had to write only a five-minute introduction and a five-minute conclusion the night before, after the specific topic was announced. A member of the committee told him afterwards that the committee had realized what he had done, but had given him the prize for thinking of doing it. That prize made it possible for Lester to enter NYU in September of that year,[9] working his way through night school to graduate in 1931 with a BA in English literature and election to Phi Beta Kappa.[10] (I still wear his key, with my own, as a pair of earrings that Rita had made.)

He also studied Latin, which he was proud of, using it later whenever he could.

Rita's Life in Vienna . . .

The confusion about Lester's country of origin (Poland? Russia? Germany?) takes another form, confusing in a different way, in the question of Rita's cultural origins. Rita Roth was born in New York City on June 9, 1911, to an Austrian Czech mother (Elsa Baruch Roth) (Figure 14) and a Hungarian father (Alex Roth, born in Kežmarok, Slovakia) (Figure 13). So Rita was a native-born US citizen. But her parents took her to Vienna shortly after her birth, and she lived there through her early years, so her first language was German (or rather, more precisely, or less precisely, Viennese); to the end of her life, Rita could only remember which months had thirty days by reciting a poem in German.

Rita was deeply traumatized by the economic hardships of her early years in Vienna, from World War I to the early 1920s. She once told me that when she was sent to market to get a hare or a rabbit, she had to make sure the head was still on, or it might be a cat. But her memories of life in the late 1920s were basically happy. The family lived on Berggasse, the street where Freud lived; Rachmaninoff once tuned their piano, she always insisted. They were quite wealthy —Alex Roth imported billiard cloth and carriage robes made of fur and fake fur—and thoroughly assimilated.

They rode horses in the Prater, had a box at the opera. (If you've read Edmund de Waal's book, *The Hare with Amber Eyes*, you've read about the culture of Rita's family. In later life, she even collected Japanese netsukes, which de Waal writes much about and referenced in the title of his book.) Rita studied at the Mädchen Gymnasium and embraced Bauhaus concepts of art and architecture; she learned to paint. She studied music and became an accomplished pianist. She knew French and Italian, as well as German and English, and was literate in them all. The gaping contrast between her life of ease in Vienna and Lester's poverty in Raczki can be seen in a glance at the photographs of them in their early childhood (Figures 17 and 3, reproduced on the cover of this book).

Rita's maternal grandmother, Franzi (Franziska) Baruch, was born on October 20, 1866, in Nova Kdyne Neugedein, in what is now the Czech Republic. Franzi had thirteen siblings, and when they were young, they used to sleep all in one large room, in separate beds. Franzi was charged with watching to make sure they didn't touch themselves: "Mama! Max has his hands under the blankets!" In about 1903, Franzi's husband, Emil Baruch, had bought the Hotel New York (as it had been called since around 1869) in Marienbad and transformed it "into a modern exquisite palace which surpassed all the surrounding hotels in terms of extraordinary façade and high dominant tower"[11] (Figure 11). On one occasion, a Russian prince, short of the cash to pay his bill, paid by giving Franzi his seven-piece harem ring, each piece adorned with a diamond, emerald, ruby, and small pearl. She kept it through the years, and Rita had it, and now I have it.

Franzi ran the hotel. She had a famously loud voice, which diners on the outside terraces could hear clearly when she was bellowing down in the kitchens, quite some distance away. On her frequent visits to the dining room, where she greeted familiar guests and checked on what the kitchen was sending out, she wore a tailored jacket, in the breast pocket of which she carried a small silver fork. She would zero in on a table where members of her family were dining, spy a particular dish, take out her fork, and plunge it into the food in question. Rita remembers protesting, "Grandmama, I[ch] bestell' dir [et]was!" (I'll order some for you!). But in vain: the fork would descend relentlessly, as Franzi muttered, "I[ich] will nur *kosten*!" (I only want to *taste* it!). This habit seems to have been passed down with the female genes, as everyone in my maternal line has always insisted on tasting, uninvited, whatever anyone else is eating.

Rita spent her summers at the hotel in Marienbad. She vividly described to me the painting on the dining room wall depicting the crowned heads of Europe promenading in front of the Colonnade, holding elaborate Czech glass tankards filled with salubrious sulfur spring waters, the famous *Brünnen*. My grandmother Elsa and my great aunt

Gretl (Elsa's sister) were also painted there in a corner, two little girls using sticks to roll their large hoop. Rita also remembered a clearing in Marienbad, where, as she wrote in her notes, "I bounced thin rubber balls that rebounded with a high-pitched boing, and I rolled my hoop."

In the summer of 1929, when Rita was eighteen, she was heard to remark, "The Czechs are hicks (*Bauern*)," and was arrested as a spy. (Like so many Viennese, Rita was a snob about both Hungarians and Czechs, though her father was Hungarian and her mother Czech. She used to say that the recipe for Hungarian goulash began, "First, steal a cow. . . .") Out on bail, Rita managed, with the help of her uncle Hans (Grandma Elsa's brother), to sneak into the woods one night and walk over the border back into Austria. But her passport was confiscated. Her grandfather, Emil Baruch, had died in Marienbad in May of that year, at the age of seventy-five. The stock market crashed that October, and Rita's father, Grandpa Roth, lost all his money. Rita never returned to Marienbad after that, for thirty years. All thirteen of Franzi's siblings died in Auschwitz in 1944. Franzi alone escaped to America.

Rita salvaged a few precious treasures from all they had to leave behind when they left Vienna. There was an ornate porcelain clock, perhaps a foot high and a foot and a half wide, consisting of a tableau with a grandfather clock (with hands that kept time, from a mechanism concealed behind it) flanked by two elegant ladies in pastel colors, white and pink and pale purple, wearing elaborate wigs and shoes, like characters in *Der Rosenkavalier*. And there were three Rosenthal figurines, each about a foot high, a white monkey and a white dog and a red fox, magically exquisite, fragile, mysterious. Rita kept them locked up in a special glass-fronted cupboard. When she died, the fox and dog and monkey were what I most wanted to inherit, for I had always felt that they were what she valued most in the world, and to this day I keep them, as she did, in a glass-fronted cupboard with my other fragile treasures. When I look at them, I am instantly transformed into the young child I was, filled with awe and amazement that anything could be so beautiful and so precious.

. . . and America

Lester and Rita occupied diametrically opposite positions in their families: he was the youngest of five children, and she was the oldest of five children. As his older siblings had cared for him, she cared for her younger siblings. After Rita, born in 1911, came Harry in 1913, then Alex Jr., called Juny, in 1916, and the twins, Elsie and Dorothy, in 1920 (Figure 15). When Rita was fifteen, in 1926, her parents divorced, and her mother left the family. Rita had to raise the children, the twins (who were six years old) and Juny and Harry (then ten and thirteen). Juny and Harry were sent to school in Oswestry, which had apparently been recommended to their father by an English merchant from whom he bought billiard cloth. They were not brought home for vacations. Once Juny got so homesick that he saved up his money and paid his fare to see his mother in Vienna. On another occasion, Harry, angry with his teacher, brought his father's gun to school, aimed it at the teacher, and pulled the trigger. Luckily, it was not loaded.

Rita tied the twins to the legs of the dining room table when she had to go out. She despised the twins, and they had twisted, conflicted, largely negative feelings about her. Over and above the mythologizing tendency that colors all of my family memories, Rita's version of most incidents that involve her and the twins differs dramatically from what I heard from them. When these differences came to light, Rita would say that both of her sisters were pathological liars.

She also resented them because they went on to college, and she did not. This was in part because she had to stay home to look after them and their brothers, but also because she never lived anywhere long enough to finish the school year. After the divorce, in 1926, Rita's father bought a big house in Great Neck, but they didn't really settle there; they made frequent trips to Vienna until 1929. Rita would have been fifteen through eighteen then, her high school years. Grandma Elsa, a Wagnerian opera singer, sang sometimes in Vienna, sometimes in New York; she dragged Rita and the twins back and forth across the Atlantic. Our attic held five or six enormous steamer trunks, some marked

"Not Wanted on Voyage" (a motto I have always kept in mind when trying to cut down things I've written), all covered with many stickers from different steamship lines. So Rita went to high school in Great Neck, but she also went to Mädchen Gymnasium in Vienna, and she didn't graduate from either, a fact that she bitterly regretted to her dying day. When her father died, in 1967, at the age of eighty-five, Rita wept but insisted that she wasn't weeping for the loss of her father—just for his wasted life. When her mother died, in 1980, aged ninety-three (Figure 21), Rita's siblings asked her to give the eulogy at the funeral, as the eldest, but Rita refused, simply stating that she couldn't think of a single good thing to say about her mother.

Their Last Year in Marienbad

Neither Lester nor Rita returned to Europe until long after World War II was over, and then it was largely for my sake. When I graduated from high school, in the summer of 1958, they took me on the European tour. We sailed on the SS *Queen Mary*, docked at Cherbourg, and went to Frankfurt, where we picked up a new car—a big, blue Mercedes 300 touring car—which we drove across Germany to Vienna, on to Marienbad, back to Paris, and eventually to Cherbourg, from which we and the Mercedes sailed back to New York.

As soon as we got to Frankfurt to pick up the car, Rita, for the first time in her life, was unable to speak. She could only produce a hoarse, barely audible whisper. Lester was clearly upset. "Rita," he said, "how are we going to manage all across Germany if you can't speak?" "You can speak," she whispered. "Speak Yiddish. They'll think you're speaking German." "They will *not*," Lester complained, "and I am not going to speak Yiddish all across Germany." But he did; it was our only option. Austria too. It made him extremely nervous. "You're doing fine," Rita would whisper to him. "They think you're speaking German." They obviously did not, but Germany and Austria were still poor, still recovering from the war, and we were driving a fancy car. Everywhere, palms were held out to be crossed with silver. There were no unpleasant incidents. Finally we left Austria, and as we crossed the border into Czechoslovakia, miraculously, Rita's voice returned. She never again, to my knowledge, displayed any other symptoms that could be interpreted as hysterical. She simply could not speak German in Germany or Austria.

We went to Marienbad (called Marianske Lazne at that time) and found the Hotel New York still standing, though now called the Polonia Hotel. (In 1950, the new owner, the Revolutionary Trade Union Movement, had renamed it.) We entered and found our way to the dining hall, and to our astonishment, there on the wall was the enormous painting with my grandmother Elsa and my great aunt Gretl with their hoop and sticks. Nervous under watchful Communist eyes, we did not take any photographs of the painting, or anything else in Marienbad. We returned to America with the Mercedes. Years later, when my niece Kate, Tony's daughter, visited Marienbad and the hotel in 2008, the painting was gone. When I visited the hotel in June 2018, the original painting was still not to be found. Yet what appear to be black and white copies of the painting hung on the walls in each of the three upper halls of the hotel. There are no crowned heads, and no *Brünnen*, but elegant ladies are still promenading in front of the Colonnade, and the little girls are there with their hoop (Figure 12).

CHAPTER TWO

Who Lester Was

When Rita introduced Lester to her grandmother, Franzi Baruch, she said, "Grandmama, isn't he handsome?" (Ist er nicht schoen?), and Franzi replied, "A man doesn't have to be handsome" (Ein Mann muss nicht schoen sein). Lester had gray-blue eyes and a sensuous mouth (Figures 8 and 10). He was not very tall (about five foot eight or nine) and tended to put on weight. (I recall him giving his size for something as "42 portly.") In later life, Lester dressed nattily but soberly in Brooks Brothers suits. His fingers were stubby, and he wore no jewelry but his wedding ring and a gold watch on an alligator leather strap. He had a distinctive warm, brown smell, a mix of toast, wood fires, and tweed. When he died, I kept his gray cashmere sweater that had his smell on it.

Beneath Lester's friendly and outgoing manner there was a darkness, a sadness that one saw in his face at times when he thought he was unobserved. He was quick-tempered, but he almost always controlled his anger, only rarely allowing himself an outburst. More often, the anger smoldered for days; he had a tendency to sulk. Yet you could tell from his face precisely what he was thinking or feeling.

His Family

Because Lester's family had come to America right after World War I, his older brothers, Jack and Simon, were well established over here long before I was born. (His sister Katy had died before I was born, and his sister Sonja lived in Sweden. I remember Sonja vividly from visits in my childhood. She spoke Swedish, and her English was rough and strongly accented. She loved clichés and truisms; I remember her often saying, "In the still waters is the woist fishes.") We saw Jack and Simon and their children from time to time (Figure 1).[12] We were closest to Simon, whose daughter Ann was just two years older than me. Because she was an only child (and I was, too, in effect), Ann was more like a sister than a cousin. We often took vacations with Ann and Simon and his wife Irma, whose brother, Leo Robin, was a successful Hollywood songwriter who wrote the lyrics for *Gentlemen Prefer Blondes* (including "Diamonds Are a Girl's Best Friend"). They hung out with Carol Channing and seemed very glamorous to me. I loved them best of all our relatives.

His Politics

My very first memory is of my father and his greatest political hero. I was four and a half years old, and Lester was sitting in the backyard on one of those folding aluminum chairs with wide bands of plastic webbing woven over the seat and the back. He was crying, which is, I think, why the moment imprinted itself on my memory so deeply; I had never seen him cry before. He picked me up and put me on his lap, and put his arms around me and said, "A very great man has died today." It was April 12, 1945, and Franklin Delano Roosevelt was dead.

Wherever Lester went, he was interested in politics. I remember squirming with embarrassment as a young girl when we went to Jamaica and, in the car that was carrying us over the hills from Kingston to Ocho Rios, Lester would say to the native driver, speaking very loudly and very slowly, "DO THE PEOPLE LIKE THEIR NEW PRESIDENT?"

Lester was a staunch patriot. He had lived the American dream, from rags to riches, and was always deeply grateful to this country for what it had done for him. As a card-carrying liberal, he was a fervent supporter of the American Civil Liberties Union. During the McCarthy period, in the early 1950s, I remember a number of occasions when the doorbell rang while we were at dinner; a man would come in, someone I didn't know, looking apologetic and worried. Lester would snatch a few hasty bites, dab his mouth with his napkin, and take the stranger upstairs to his study. An hour or so later, they would come downstairs, often laughing together, and I would hear the man say, "How can I ever thank you?" Lester would say, "Nonsense, it's really nothing; you'll be back on your feet soon, I know you will." I never knew exactly what he gave them — money? A job? Advice? All three? But years later, total strangers would come up to me when they heard that my name was Doniger, and would tell me that Lester had saved their careers, often their families, at that time.

He remained active in Democratic politics, a Stevenson man and then a Kennedy man. He was also involved with Planned Parenthood and SIECUS (Sexuality Information and Education Council of the United States), which he joined when Mary Calderone founded it in 1964; he became president of SIECUS in 1968. As a result of these various activities, pages of the Congressional Record in 1967 were filled with slander about Lester (some of it from guilt by association with Rita).[13] They said he was born in Russia — aha! — and that he later denied it, saying that he had been born in Poland — aha! aha! — and that his wife was a known Communist, and so forth.

When I think of Lester's politics, I think of his generosity, but also of his tact and his skill in winning people over to his way of thinking. He taught me a lesson about all that when I was very little indeed but already plagued by the sharp impatience that is my curse to this day. When we were driving in the car, I hated waiting for red lights to change, and I undoubtedly became quite tedious about it. Lester then taught me a sure-fire bit of magic that *inevitably* made red lights turn to green: you simply introduced yourself politely and explained to the lights, calmly and slowly, why it was that you wanted them to change. So this is how it went: "Red light, please change to green. My name is Wendy Doniger, and I am a friend of red lights. We are on our way to visit my grandparents. We're already quite late, because Mommy took forever in packing up the presents, and Grandma will be worried — she's very old, and lives in Brooklyn . . ." and sure enough, soon the red light changed to green. It never failed.

His Religion

Lester's father was a pious and learned man, a Talmudic scholar who adhered to Jewish law in all things and, when they first came to America, taught Hebrew for a while. When Lester was a boy, in Russia, whenever they were having a *fleischig* (meat) meal, his mother would call him into the kitchen (ostensibly to help her with something), put her finger over her mouth to signal secrecy, and give him a glass of milk, for she believed that a growing child should drink milk with every meal, *fleischig* or not. Lester as an adult kept no dietary laws; he ate shrimp and bacon (even when they were not part of Chinese food). But on one occasion, when he had ordered a roast beef sandwich in a delicatessen and it came with butter on it, he made the only fuss I ever saw him make in a restaurant, where he was usually characteristically thoughtful to the staff. This time he was truly upset, and I think it came from some deep sympathy with his father's horror of mixing *milchig* (dairy) and *fleischig*.

Though a confirmed nonobservant atheist, Lester was nevertheless very serious about being a Jew. According to his obituary in the *New York Times*, he contributed generously to our local Temple Beth-el and served on its board; he supported B'nai B'rith, and was a director of the American Jewish Congress. Rita regarded this as reprehensible hypocrisy. During our interview with NPR long after his death, she said, "Lester was a Jew. But he wasn't a religious Jew. He never went to the Jewish ceremonies, because he didn't believe in it. However, it was important to Lester that everybody should love him. So I found out later that he contributed a lot of money to the Jews." He sent money to Israel, too, but though both Tony and I visited Israel, Lester never did. I remember arriving in Tel Aviv on my first visit, after Lester had died, and being asked, "What was your father's name?" and bursting into tears.

We celebrated Christmas (in a secular way: the tree and the presents, but not the Midnight Mass) rather than Hanukkah (though we sometimes did have a Menorah, and more presents), and we usually went to Passover seders at Jack's house, though we never ever hosted one ourselves —Rita would not have known how and would not have been willing to learn. When I was in my early twenties, during a visit home from Harvard, where I was studying Sanskrit and Greek, when the dinner table was cleared, Lester sat down with my brother Tony. They were reading together. "What are you doing?" I asked. "Teaching Tony

Hebrew," Lester replied. "You know Hebrew?" I asked, idiotically, but truly I was amazed. "Of course I know Hebrew," he replied. "Why didn't you teach *me* Hebrew?" I asked, my voice rising. "You never asked me," he replied, which was true enough. It had never occurred to me. I had never heard Lester speak a word of Hebrew, except at seders (where even I knew the words of the basic prayers, which were always transcribed into Roman letters in the sort of watered-down, contemporary, politically correct Haggadahs that we used). He was so secular that he never used his Hebrew, but he was so traditional that he could not imagine teaching a *girl* Hebrew.

Lester was preparing Tony for his Bar Mitzvah. It later transpired that Tony, also relentlessly secular then and ever after, had not wanted a Bar Mitzvah. This is how Tony tells the story in a 2015 email: "Here is my very clear recollection: I didn't want to go through all the work (and miss all that baseball playing time) to get Bar Mitzvah, and I said so when Lester raised the issue; Rita supported me, for her own reasons; a compromise was struck between us that I would go to Temple Beth-el Sunday school for one year and then decide if I wanted to continue — if I didn't I would be tutored in the evenings by a retired rabbi. That's what happened, only the rabbi died within a few months of tutorials; so Lester took over, but that didn't last very long at all, and eventually the effort was dropped. But when my thirteenth birthday approached Lester suggested in the strongest terms that I should have a big birthday party, which I thought was a great idea; it only dawned on me as an adult that everyone would have thought this was a post–Bar Mitzvah party and they simply hadn't been invited to the ceremony, thus preserving the appearance Lester desired (not me) of his Jewish household."

So Rita had a point about Lester's Jewish hypocrisy.

Tony forgot his Hebrew within months of his non–Bar Mitzvah. At Radcliffe, and then Harvard, I had taken courses in Jewish history with Hayim Hillel Ben Sasson. I finally studied Hebrew years later, when I was in my fifties and teaching in Chicago, and I did learn enough to read the texts I needed for a book I was writing,[14] though I forgot most of it after a while. But Tony (who, like me, married a Christian and celebrates both Christmas and Hanukkah) does sometimes go to Temple on Yom Kippur, to maintain some connection with his (and Lester's) Jewish roots. Tony is thus truly carrying on the spirit of Lester's Judaism.

Lester was very much a Jew in his attitude to antisemitism. When I was six or seven, we lived a few blocks away from the Johnsons, who were immigrants from Sweden; Mr. Johnson was a carpenter. One day when I was walking past their house, the Johnson children threw stones at me and shouted at me. Frightened more than hurt, but badly frightened and even more bewildered, I ran home and told Lester what had happened. And I asked him, "Daddy, why is it bad to be called a kite?" He didn't answer, but strode darkly out of the house. He returned after half an hour or so and told me that the Johnson children would not bother me anymore, and they never did. I never discovered what he had done — talked to them? Talked to their parents? Threatened them? Punished them? Nor do I remember what, if anything, he told me about kikes.

His Books and Music

In his youth, Lester had ambitions of becoming a writer. He once wrote a short story, entitled "The Rejection Letter," about the dire consequences that followed, both for the writer and for the magazine in question, on one occasion when such a letter was sent. He sent his story to the *New Yorker*, which sent it back with a rejection letter, saying they would take their chances. After that, he stuck to editing and publishing, but he always regretted that he had not become a novelist, or at least an author of books, himself.

Lester's literary tastes were classical and serious. He loved big books: Thomas Wolfe (who had been his teacher at NYU) and Thomas Hardy, and Galsworthy, and Dos Passos, and James Gould Cozzens's *By Love Possessed*. He especially loved big Russian books, which he read in translation, generally preferring the quasi-tsarist to the quasi-Revolutionary: Tolstoy more than Dostoyevsky, Chekhov more than Bulgakov, but Sholokhov more than Nabokov. He would come home from the office at about 5:00 p.m.

each day, his top shirt button and the knot of his tie loosened, carrying his jacket neatly folded over his arm, and holding a couple of books under his other arm. Often they were advance copies, sometimes long galleys, of books he was considering for one of his book clubs, or just books that interested him. (Two books a day, three hundred fifty days a year, added up, and we kept building new bookcases.) As soon as he came in, he called out "Hello," then made himself a Scotch sour (I always got to eat the slice of orange and the maraschino cherry), settled himself into his armchair in the living room, and opened one of the books he had brought home. I remember his excitement when he came home with an advance copy of *Dr. Zhivago*, in 1958.

His musical tastes were simple. He liked Brahms and Tchaikovsky and Martita Hunt's recording of Bach's *Well-Tempered Clavier*. He particularly loved the cello; he was a great fan of Pablo Casals, whom he often traveled to hear, to Marlboro, Vermont, and occasionally Puerto Rico. In his later years, Lester decided to take up the cello himself, though he had never played a musical instrument, not even the piano or a guitar. Leonard Rose, who lived near us and was a close friend, helped him buy a cello and came to the house to give him lessons, but it soon became cruelly obvious to all of us that Lester was entirely tone deaf; he had no idea when he was playing the wrong note. Leonard Rose gently discouraged him, and, sadly, he gave away the cello.

Lester loved the simpler operas, the ones where you came home humming a tune, *Carmen* and *La Bohème* and *La Traviata*, and especially *Cavalleria Rusticana* and *Pagliacci* (known as *Cav* and *Pag*). He used to joke that *Pagliacci* was the only opera that dealt with antisemitism: "Invest in the Jewboy" (Vesti la giubba). He did not care at all for Wagner. His favorite singer was Ezio Pinza, whose sweet, low, warm, fatherly voice always, to this day, reminds me of Lester.

The Story of Pulpit Digest

When Lester graduated from NYU, in 1931, he got a job as a stringer on the religion page of the *New York Times*, visiting the major churches in Manhattan every Sunday and summarizing the sermons; he was paid by the inch. (My brother Tony thinks it was the *New York World*.) Eventually it dawned on Lester that it might be profitable to serve as a kind of (Jewish) matchmaker between those Protestant ministers who yearned to see their sermons in print, publicly, and those Protestant ministers who were eager to have at their disposal every week, privately, the sermons of the first sort of ministers. And so he founded, in May 1936, *Pulpit Digest*, an interdenominational journal for the American Protestant clergy.

At that time he was courting Rita, and at the start, *Pulpit Digest* was a family affair. He ran off copies at home on stencils that printed in purple, and Rita addressed the envelopes. Often the two of them wrote some of the sermons themselves, together. It was their plan, Rita's idea (she later claimed), to write sermons on topics of political and social importance, arguing both sides of every question, and to write them in terms so general that any clergyman — rabbi, minister, or priest — could preach them. (Lester and Rita had also contemplated starting another journal, *Pro and Con*, in which they would argue both sides of every important political issue.) So they wrote, under various pseudonyms, sermons that were preached all over America by Protestant clergymen who little dreamed that their homilies had been composed by two European Jews. The family connection persisted: on the cover of the May 1949 issue of *Pulpit Digest* is a picture of me, then eight years old, in pigtails, sitting in the sun in Rita's daisy patch, over a stanza from the *Song of Songs*: "For, lo! The winter is past, the rain is over and gone . . ." (Figure 6).

In 1950 Lester began to publish *Pastoral Psychology* (edited by his brother Simon, who had completed a PhD in social work and education from NYU in 1939). Soon both journals attracted leaders in the field of religion. The very first issue of *Pastoral Psychology*, in 1950, had articles by Lawrence S. Kubie, Rollo May, and Norman Vincent Peale. The June 1954 issue of *Pulpit Digest* (vol. 34, no. 194), a special issue devoted to "The Hydrogen-Cobalt Bomb," included messages from Bertrand Russell, Martin Buber, Dag Hammarskjöld, Jawaharlal Nehru, Eleanor Roosevelt,

Norman Thomas, and Paul Tillich. And the January 1956 issue of *Pastoral Psychology* published a letter that C. G. Jung had written to Simon Doniger, entitled "Why and How I Wrote My *Answer to Job*."[15] There is, in Martin Luther King's papers, a letter from him to *Pulpit Digest*, dated November 27, 1959, politely declining an invitation to write a sermon for Race Relations Sunday, to be printed in *Pulpit Digest*. (Lester was always a staunch supporter of Martin Luther King. I cherish a book inscribed to him from King.)

Along the way, Lester began to publish books. He founded Channel Press and the Book Club Guild, making Ralph Raughley (an old friend of Rita's) his vice president (Figure 4). He published a number of good books, such as *Lincoln's Devotional* (with an introduction by Carl Sandburg) in 1957, and *Really, Not Really*, by Robert Frost's daughter Lesley, in 1962. Rarely, Lester's timing was off. He had the bright idea of publishing a book called *Letters to Mother*, a collection of letters by famous men to their moms, to be published in time for Mother's Day, 1959. The editor's preface said, "Napoleon ruled the world, but his letters to maman begged her to help him rule his family. What would I find, I wondered, in other letters to mothers written by other despots, by scientists and soldiers, by princesses and poets? The result is, I think, a unique view of many fascinating people." The editor was Charles Van Doren, a man both widely respected — a professor of literature at Columbia University, scion of a famous literary

family (son of Mark Van Doren) — and one of the first public intellectuals, a television star on a quiz program called
Twenty One. Alas, on November 2, 1959, Van Doren admitted to a United States Congress subcommittee that he had
been given questions and answers in advance of the show.
The resulting scandal (immortalized in the 1994 film *Quiz
Show*, in which Ralph Fiennes played Van Doren) was sudden death for a book — published just a few months earlier — about being nice to your mother. We had piles of
remaindered copies in an upstairs closet. (Years later, I got
to know Van Doren when we served together on the International Board of the *Encyclopædia Britannica*, under Mor-
timer Adler. We never discussed *Twenty-One* or, for that
matter, *Letters to Mother*.)

How to Be Accepted by the College of Your Choice, by Benjamin Fine (1957), was a winner. And so was *Watch Your
Language* (1958), based on a collection of the "winners and
sinners" memos that Ted Bernstein, chief copy editor at
the *New York Times*, sent out every week, noting particularly good and bad writing in the paper. (It had a preface by
Jacques Barzun, who was also on the *Encyclopædia Britannica* board with me, and remembered Lester quite fondly.)
Lester would publish books like these that he knew would
make money, in order to publish others that he feared
might lose money, such as Upton Sinclair's lightly fiction-
alized temperance diatribe, *The Cup of Fury* (1956). Lester
admired the French novelist Loys Masson and published

English translations of two of his books — *The Shattered Sexes* (1961) and *The Tortoises* (1962) — that *no one* bought. Masson's books inhabited the closet next to the Van Doren book, which, unlike Masson's, had been slated to be a moneymaker. Lester called this balancing process robbing Peter to pay Paul.

The ecclesiastical metaphor is appropriate, as the business was from the start anchored in Christianity. Lester invented the Ministers' Dollar Book Club and developed a mailing list of just about all the Protestant ministers in America. Through that base, he was active in interfaith movements and generally hung out with the dog-collar crowd. Samuel McCrea Cavert, long a driving force in the World Council of Churches, was an editor of *Pulpit Digest* and a cherished family friend. I have a photograph I have always thought of as "Daddy and the Bishop": there is Lester, looking so young, with a rather strained smile on his face, accepting from some stunningly ecclesiastical-looking WASP (identified on the back of the photograph as "Bishop Sherrill, Presiding Bishop Episcopal Church") a plaque on behalf of *Pulpit Digest* (Figure 5). I didn't know the phrase "token Jew" in those days, or the concept of what Sir Isaiah Berlin called the "court Jew," and indeed Lester was more than that, but I think, in retrospect, that he was that, too. He was so comfortable within the Protestant world that he could make insider jokes; he used to joke that Unitarians prayed "to whom it may concern," and that when you dialed the Unitarian "Dial-a-Prayer" number, nobody answered.

When John F. Kennedy was running for president, in 1960, the conservative activist H. L. Hunt Jr. got ahold of Lester's mailing lists at a time when Lester was vacationing away from the office. Hunt sent out a rabid anti-Catholic pamphlet, using the address format that immediately identified it as a *Pulpit Digest* mailing. When Lester found out about this, he was appalled, and was preparing to send out a statement to all his subscribers, insisting that he had had nothing to do with the mailing and abhorred such sentiments, when the letters started pouring in — thanking him for getting on board the move to keep a Catholic out of the White House. Lester was so disgusted with his subscribers that he decided then and there to get rid of the business. He sold the whole business, the Book Club Guild and *Pulpit Digest* and all the rest, sometime after 1965, when Meredith Press approached him with a very profitable offer, largely because Lester's business was on the cutting edge of computerization. But he also had another reason to sell the company: he had had a mild heart attack (though ultimately he died not of that but of cancer), and he didn't want Tony to feel that he had to take over the family business.

Both Simon and Lester retired in 1969, but *Pulpit Digest* continued, out of Louisville, Kentucky, until well into the 1980s,[16] and *Pastoral Psychology* is still going strong.

CHAPTER THREE

Who Rita Was

Rita had red hair and deep-set green eyes and a noble, Roman nose, strong features that always reminded me of Greer Garson. She took great care of her appearance, applying lipstick with a brush, carefully outlining her lips and then filling them in. She plucked her brows, used green eye shadow and black mascara, and dyed her hair red after she had begun to go gray. She dressed with Viennese elegance, with jewelry and silk scarves and hats. She always wore Schiaparelli "Shocking" perfume, which came in a bottle shaped like a dressmaker's mannequin. When I grew old enough to wear perfume, I asked if I too could wear "Shocking," but she refused: a little girl should not smell like her mother. When I was in college, I had a wealthy boyfriend who gave me, for Christmas, a large bottle of Jean Patou's "Joy," then (and perhaps still) the most expensive perfume in the world. Rita made big eyes at it and finally offered to trade me her half-empty bottle of "Shocking" for my brand-new bottle of "Joy." I agreed, and wore "Shocking" for many years after that, until they stopped making it.

Rita was always, until she became old, quite plump. (She wrote in her notes, "I am engaged in a great civil war, ego vs. id, appetite vs. avoirdupois.") She could make her belly do a belly dance by flexing the muscles. But she dressed very well. She had two large walk-in closets full of clothes. She had kept everything she ever wore, from the early days in Vienna to the latest fashions, assuring me that it would all come back into style, as indeed most of it did. Years later, I was reminded of the chronological layers of her closet when I discovered that Hinduism, like Rita, never threw anything out: Sanskrit texts kept, side by side, like Rita's dresses, ancient ideas and more recent ideas that contradicted them and that might, in another religion, have replaced them.

Rita was what was then called a housewife (nowadays a "homemaker"), but on her applications for passports and so forth she always put, under "occupation," "beachcomber." She was notoriously eccentric in the ways she dressed, expressed her opinions, and decorated the house. (She put on the downstairs powder room door a sign she had stolen from somewhere: "Deliver All Goods Through Rear.") She loved animals and had a knack for training them. She taught our cat, Mrs. Pussycat, to use the toilet. She could look a dachshund in the eye (we always had dachshunds) and say, in a loud voice, "*Hund!*" and the dog did whatever she told it to do.

She was a great trickster. She had a convincingly lifelike plastic replica of a big slice of Gouda cheese that she used to place on the cheese tray in the midst of all the real cheese, and would enjoy the look on the face of the hapless guest who tried to slice into it. She felt that nothing was off-limits, that you could joke about absolutely everything. She believed in what she called *Galgenhumor*, gallows humor, which *Merriam-Webster* defines as "humor that relates to very serious or frightening things (such as death and illness)" and the (anti-German) *Oxford English Dictionary* defines as "grim, ironical humour; 'sick' humour." The Viennese, with their ever-present diminutive ending "l" (as in Hans-l and Gret-l) miniaturized everything, and death, horror, and tragedy were no exceptions. Wiktionary defines *Galgenhumor* as "comedy that still manages to be funny in the face of a perfectly hopeless situation." This is the definition that fits Rita best; she felt that *Galgenhumor* was a particularly Viennese trait, and she told a story that exemplified, she said, the difference between the Germans and the Viennese. The story was about the very end of World War II, Hitler in the bunker, the Allies closing in on Berlin. The Nazis in Berlin sent a telegram to the Nazis in Vienna, saying that the situation in Berlin was "ernst aber nicht hoffnungslos" (serious but not hopeless). The Viennese replied that, on the contrary, the situation in Vienna was "hoffnungslos aber nicht ernst" (hopeless but not serious). That joke, embodying the situation that it imagines, is pure *Galgenhumor*. For Rita, nothing was ever too serious to joke about.

Rita never told a lie, not even the ordinary white lies that smooth over the bumps in human relationships. Trying, in vain, to convert me to this philosophy, she would argue, "If you don't lie, you don't have to remember what you said," which is of course true. When I persisted in telling lies, she washed my mouth out with soap. I can still remember clenching my teeth against the rigid pressure, and the taste of the soap on my tongue. She never compromised. When, as a child, I would show her my amateurish drawings from school, she never praised them but pointed out their flaws. If someone gave her as a present a book she already had, she said she already had it, or, if the gift was a scarf, and she never wore that color, she said she never wore that color. She did not sugarcoat her responses to unwelcome invitations; she wrote in her notes, "Of course one avoids dining with people one doesn't like or enjoy. One can always say politely, 'I am going to be ill' or 'I'm not hungry, thank you.'" And indeed, I remember an occasion when a neighbor she didn't like persisted in asking Rita, months in advance, to a Bar Mitzvah she had no intention of attending. Rita finally simply said, "I plan to be ill on that day."

Rita believed in complete integrity and originality. She would never let me color in outlines or connect the dots, but insisted that I draw what was in my own mind and eye. And when she made petit-point embroidery, she used her own highly original designs rather than the ready-made sketches that other women followed. She would never do anything just because other people did it or because you were supposed to do it. This made her a scofflaw; she broke the law constantly, and I was often her unwilling and nervous accomplice. She regarded a stop sign as a suggestion rather than a command, and parked wherever she liked no matter what the signs said. When driving, she never paid any attention to speed limits. In those days long before seat belts, let alone children's car seats, she stationed me kneeling on the back seat, looking out the back window to see if any cops were following us. She always carried with her a trowel with which she dug up other people's plants, insisting that they regarded them as weeds; again, I was stationed as the lookout. She stole towels from hotels and smuggled shamelessly, not just the things that otherwise law-abiding people often smuggled (small purchases of liquor and perfume and so forth), but other sorts of contraband. Once she insisted on importing, on our return from a vacation in Jamaica, a rare plant that she wanted to replant in her garden, roots and all. As our flight approached New York, she threaded the flowering top through the opening at the neck of my blouse, the stem going under my blouse and secured with a belt around my waist, the roots wrapped in wet cloths covered with a plastic bag that hung down under my skirt. Apparently, it seemed to be a corsage I was wearing as I trotted innocently past the US Customs and Border Protection officers at LaGuardia, like a ten-year-old drug mule.

Rita was always late. Indeed, she regarded it as a matter

of national (Viennese) pride, often saying, as the Viennese were notorious for saying, "Komm i net heut, komm i morgen" (If I don't come today, I'll come tomorrow). Rita despised the Germans for making all the trains run on time, and she admired the Viennese, who had, in the main Vienna train station (she always insisted), an announcement board that told when the train was due and then had a second column labeled "Wie Spät" (How Late). Rita and Lester quarreled often about time, he always early and impatient, she always late and laid back.

Dinners were notoriously late, both family dinners and dinner parties, often an hour late, but occasionally two or even three hours late. Sometimes Rita was waiting for something to defrost, sometimes meat to roast or a dessert to set, but in any case it was not ready. At family dinnertime, with no food in sight, we would nibble on this and that and talk and read while we waited. Sometimes Lester would send out for a pizza or delicatessen food or Chinese food, and by the time dinner was served, no one had any appetite left; so we'd save Rita's dinner to eat, reheated, the next night, when at least it would be on time. At dinner parties, people ate peanuts and drank cocktails, and a second cocktail, and a third, often getting unintentionally tight, or they nipped out to run a short errand (or get a snack) and returned still in good time before we sat down at table.

By the time I was in high school, Rita would stay up all night and go to bed in the morning; she'd stay in bed most of the day and get up in the late afternoon to shop and prepare dinner. This continued throughout her life. Years later, when I was living in Chicago and found myself, at 3:00 a.m., in the midst of an argument about the names of the Seven Dwarfs (my interlocutor insisted that there was a dwarf named Sleazy, and I seriously doubted that), I phoned her. She answered. I said, "Hi, Mom. What are the names of the Seven Dwarfs?" and she replied, "Sleepy, Sneezy, Happy, Dopey, Grumpy, Bashful, and Doc." "Thanks, Mom," I said. "Goodnight," she said, and rang off. It seemed perfectly normal to her to have such a conversation at that hour, and she was the ideal final court of appeal, like the *Encyclopædia Britannica*, in those dark days before Google.

What did she do all night? Most important to her, I think, was the fact of simply being alone, away from all of us. (She also found solitude in the enormous raspberry patch in the middle of her large and beautiful garden. She'd disappear into the patch in June and emerge in late August, with buckets of raspberries that she froze and made into jam. The raspberry patch was so thick and brambly that none of us could find our way through the maze to get her out; she came out every evening when she was good and ready.) But at night, a lot of the time she sorted things out, obsessively arranging them and writing lists of what linen was on each shelf, what jars of preserves were in each cupboard. She would fold contour sheets. She also worked on five-thousand-piece jigsaw puzzles that she had laid out on the billiard table or Ping-Pong table in the downstairs game room, in either case a table on which, thereafter, no one ever played billiards or Ping-Pong. Uncompromising as ever, Rita only did the puzzles that had *no picture* to give you a leg up. Sometimes she did Double-Crostics, and taught me to do them too (great training for someone who would go on to translate Sanskrit, balancing lexical knowledge with the seat-of-the-pants instinct of what the passage was about). From time to time, she had company at night: my boyfriend of the moment would bring me home at a reasonable hour, whereupon I would say good night and go up to bed; but seeing Rita there, the guy would often sit down and talk with her, sometimes for hours. In later life, she would watch movies on television, staying with the *Late Late Show* until they played the national anthem and flew the American flag. Then she would go up to bed. In much later life, I would often stay up with her and watch movies all night, a habit I still have.

Like most Viennese, Rita drank coffee all day; she always had a pot of it on the stove, refreshed from time to time during the day as people stopped by. But she seldom drank wine or liquor. When I got old enough to ask her why, she said that she did not trust herself, did not know what she would do under the influence. This resolution, however, once came in conflict with her determination never to pass up a free gift. When we flew to Jamaica, back in the 1950s, after landing we waited under a lean-to made of thatched palm leaves while Jamaican workers carried the luggage out of the plane, piece by piece, on their heads (as I perhaps wrongly recall). And while we were waiting, they served us free Planter's Punches, made with Jamaican rum, of course. Rita, who could not ignore this giveaway, had several and became gloriously tight, singing Jamaican songs loudly and well. When we returned to Jamaica years later, and Lester, always trying to make friends with working people, recognized some of the staff and greeted them and then said, "But of course you would not remember any of us," one of the staff pointed at Rita and said, "I remember *her*!"

Her Family

Rita's mother, Elsa Roth, and Elsa's siblings (my great uncle Hans and my great aunt Margaret — called, of course, Hänsl and Gretl) and their spouses and children had settled in America later than Rita had. Unlike Rita, who spoke English with no accent, they all had strong Viennese accents and spoke nonidiomatic English. Rita commented on this in her notes: "*Everyone* had an accent. Nobody spoke like the parents of my schoolmates and friends. Even my parents spoke with what my mother insisted on calling an 'inflection' — This to her ears was a matter of degree, but so were all the accents — some absolutely unintelligible, some charming, some exaggerated like the protagonists of jokes acted out in vaudeville or told ineptly by chauvinistic children of chauvinistic parents."

Rita's family were in and out of our house all during my childhood; several of them lived in Great Neck or nearby, in Elmhurst or Jackson Heights or Flushing, or in New Jersey (Figure 16). Franzi Baruch, my great grandmother, lived with us until I was two or three, when she was in her late seventies. Rita's brother Juny (Alex Jr.) had been in love with a girl who turned him down, but the girl's mother had persuaded him to marry her other daughter, and he did. The marriage was not a success, and he joined the Merchant Marine Corps, stationed primarily in Guam, and was seldom seen anywhere near the Atlantic Coast.

But we saw all the others quite a lot. My uncle Harry, who lived in New Jersey and sold jewelry, visited us often. As she saw him approaching the house, Rita would summon me, or Tony, or both of us, and instruct us to stick to Harry like glue as he wandered through the house. Otherwise, she knew, he would pick up things and put them in his pocket, muttering that he was taking them "back," implying that he had either given or sold them to her. Her sister Elsie, too, would come to the house almost every day, and though she never actually took anything, she would stare at some of the things salvaged from Vienna, particularly the porcelain clock with the two courtly ladies, and remark, "Grandmama always wanted *me* to have that." (After Rita died, I saw the porcelain clock in Elsie's house. It irked me, because I knew that Rita had wanted *me* to have it. I do, after all, have the acquisitive Baruch-Roth blood in my veins.)

Often when I had a gentleman caller, my grandmother Elsa used to humiliate me by insisting on singing an operatic aria for us in a very loud voice with an out-of-control vibrato. Mortally embarrassed, I kept trying to end it, saying, "Thank you, Grandmama" at every pause in the music, and the boy would mutter, "Thank you so much, Mrs. Roth," but she went on and on and on to the bitter end.

Her Politics

Rita was not just a Communist but a Stalinist. She was a Communist simply because she believed that the rich should be forced to share their wealth with the poor. She wanted to change the world. I was a Red Diaper baby; I grew up thinking that "Trotskyite" was a dictionary term that meant "no-good son-of-a-bitch," rather than a slur based on the name of an actual person. And it was not until I went to kindergarten that I learned that there was such a thing as paper white on both sides; I had done my early drawings on the backs of flyers for Henry Wallace and Ella Winter and Russian War Relief, later Alger Hiss, and still later, the Rosenbergs. During the McCarthy era, people like Pete Seeger and Zero Mostel drifted in and out of our house. I learned my first Sanskrit words from Seeger, in Gandhi's song "Raghupati Raghava." Rita sent me to Shaker Village Work Camp in New Lebanon, New York, run on classical Communist principles, where I again encountered Pete Seeger. Under Rita's influence, I threw myself into the world of political activism. I was vice president of the Great Neck chapter of the World Communist Youth organization. Peter Camejo was the president; years later, he ran for governor of California on the Green Party ticket, and in 2004 was Ralph Nader's running mate.

Rita never wavered in her allegiance, no matter what Stalin did. When, in 1939, Stalin signed the nonaggression pact with Hitler, Rita went to bed for two days (Lester reported). On the third day, she came downstairs and said, "Stalin did what he had to do," and she remained a Stalinist. But she never actually joined the American Communist Party, for, she said, they would tell her what to do and she wouldn't do it and they would throw her out. When I brought back from Moscow, in 1971, a bust of Lenin as a gift for her, she put it in a place of honor, but with a sign she had stolen from someplace, saying, "Temporarily Out of Service."

When we were interviewed by NPR during Rita's final days, when her mind often wandered, she said to me, "You know, Trotsky may have been right about some things." And then she mused further on her Communism. "There would be no millionaires. . . . The earth should be shared. . . . And that's how it started out. . . . But they changed. How could they have changed, and become like other people, like all the rest? . . . Stalin simply killed anyone who didn't agree with him, and that was wrong. And so I lost my hope. I had hoped originally that Communism would spread and everything would become free and generous . . ."

Her Religion

There were constant reminders of the family's former glory. Rita's father, my grandfather Alex Roth, always wore a gorgeous stickpin in his tie; one had a large opal surrounded by diamonds and sapphires, another a tiny enamel portrait of the empress Elisabeth, framed by diamonds and rubies. But the older generation had not been able to establish a solid economic base here. (The one exception was Gretl, who supported herself by making exquisite round jewel cases out of Chinese silk brocade, lined with silk velvet, and sold them through Henri Bendel.) I knew that Lester was supporting most of Rita's older relatives, and that they were therefore very much in his debt. They hung around the house a lot, frequently lingering until they had to be asked to stay for dinner. Grandpa Roth visited us frequently until his death in 1967. I am told that when I was very young, perhaps four or five, I looked out of the window to see him coming up the front path and called out, "Hide the liquor, here comes the old man," a phrase I was evidently parroting from my father. It was an awkward moment.

Even as a young child, I could see that, despite the fact

that Lester was supporting most of Rita's relatives, they did not speak of him with respect. At the time I thought it was because they still maintained the aristocratic attitude they had enjoyed when they were living high on the hog in Vienna, and I think there was some truth in that. But only later, when I learned a bit about the history of the Jews, did I realize that Rita's family looked down on Lester because they were German Jews, *yekkes*, and he was an *ostjude*, a Jew from Eastern Europe. You can learn the essence of this truth in a minute just by looking at the photographs of Lester as a child in Russia and Rita as a child in Vienna (Figures 3 and 17).

More particularly, Rita's family were *yekkes* that had become thoroughly assimilated to the non-Jewish Viennese. They intermarried with Catholics and generally identified themselves as Viennese, not as Jews. Many of Rita's cousins stayed in Vienna even after the Anschluss, confident that Hitler did not mean *them*. He did, of course, and many of them died in Theresienstadt or Auschwitz. Rita, ever perverse, fully acknowledged her own Jewishness only when it became potentially fatal to admit to being a Jew. She used to say, "Hitler made me a Jew." Her mother, Elsa Roth, had actually become a Christian Scientist, and raised Rita that way. ("God is love, there is no pain," Rita used to chant from time to time, when she was in pain.)

But of course when Rita became a Communist, she renounced that, too. During our NPR interview later in her life, she assigned a much earlier date to her atheism: "By the time I was in sixth or seventh grade I began thinking and thinking and thinking, and I realized, of course there's no such thing as a god. I realized this as a little child." Her dislike of religion was entirely ecumenical: though she particularly disapproved of Catholics (because they had a list of books you could not read! — her idea of heresy), she was basically against any organization that told you what to think, and that is what she thought all religions did. She wrote in her notes: "Christianity was once in the position of communism, an unwelcome ideology . . . I still feel the way the Romans did about Christianity. I am against it. It threatens my personal philosophy and way of life. I am adamantly opposed to dogma and dogmatic doctrines." She used to say that the world would not be safe until the last rabbi was strangled with the entrails of the last priest. When, in 1954, under Joseph McCarthy, the phrase "under God" was inserted in the pledge of allegiance, Rita wouldn't let me say it, and I had to go and sit in the principal's office each day during the assembly in which all the other children said the pledge of allegiance.

The rabbis, in particular, drove her crazy. One of her best party tricks was her imitation of Rabbi (Jacob) Rudin of our local reform temple, Temple Beth-el: she brilliantly mimicked his pomposity, his ornate oratory style, the rhythmic repetition of rhetorical resonances, the pauses before certain words to give them importance — she caught him dead to rights. Yet she was a passionate opponent of anti-semitism. As she mentioned in our NPR interview, she was convinced that nine out of ten of "the very fashion-able and stylish" English detective writers were antisemitic, "because the Jews [in their books] yell loud and have big mouths and are ugly, all of them. . . . It's only the ones who are Jewish who turn out to be nasty and mean."

Her Books and Music and Paintings

Unlike Lester, whose literary tastes ran to the old-fashioned and solid, Rita favored whimsy. She was a great reader of Lewis Carroll, Max Beerbohm, Lafcadio Hearn, Edith Sitwell, and Christopher Morley. She idolized Ger-trude Stein and Arthur Conan Doyle, claiming to base her own methods on those of Sherlock Holmes. ("You see, Watson, but you do not observe!" she would intone to me, whenever I didn't follow her reasoning.)

Music was what she cared about most. As soon as she woke up, she turned on the radio, WQXR, and it stayed on until she went to sleep. When I awoke I would listen, and if there was music, she was up. Saturday afternoons, we lis-tened to the Metropolitan Opera broadcasts, with Milton Cross announcing. Rita had a music system installed with speakers in every room playing the radio or whatever re-cord she put on the record player, so that she could hear it wherever she went in the house. Not only could she identify any piece she heard on the radio, anything from

Palestrina to John Cage, but she would tell you the singers, the soloists, the conductor, and all the orchestral first chairs, as well as the year in which the recording was made. Opera was her favorite, especially Wagner and Richard Strauss, and she was a great admirer of the famous Viennese interpreter of Strauss, Elisabeth Schwarzkopf, particularly beloved for her portrayal of the Marschallin in *Der Rosenkavalier*. When Rita's Jewish friends protested that Schwarzkopf had been intimately connected with members of the Nazi high command, and urged her not to patronize Schwarzkopf's performances, Rita replied, "I regard her singing as reparations for my cousins who died in Auschwitz." But Rita was eclectic in everything, even music. Once, when I asked her who she thought was the greatest living singer, expecting Schwarzkopf or Jussi Bjoerling or Maria Callas, she replied, "Louis Armstrong." She was also a great fan of Billie Holiday. She played the piano herself, brilliantly and uncompromisingly — no matter how difficult the piece was, she played it at the appropriate tempo, without stopping, even if that meant that she made mistakes. When I practiced the piano, Czerny and Kabalevsky and stuff that Mozart wrote when he was two, and invariably made a mistake, no matter where she was in the house, Rita shouted, "Falsch!" (Wrong!)

She had a wonderful collection of Indian art, which she began buying in the late 1950s, when I had started to study India and Lester had started to make a lot of money. Her

favorite was Ganesha — the elephant-headed god of intellectuals, particularly beloved to her because he was fat and
held a ball of food (sweets) in one of his several hands. She
bought a number of Ganeshas in New York, and when she
visited me in India (Figure 32), she managed to find and buy
many strange and beautiful things, including several Ganeshas, in just the short time she was there. She loved Japanese art, and had a fabulous collection of the little ivory
carvings known as netsukes. Rita had an unerring eye. Despite her deep bias against religion, she appreciated religious
art, and bought — when they were bargains — a fourteenth-
century Spanish triptych depicting the martyrdom of Saint
Stephen, and a Madonna from the Riemenschneider atelier.
Rita was also fascinated by the Buddhist and Hindu friezes
at Angkor Wat (she pronounced it "Angkor Vat," which I
took to be its name until, much later, I began to read about
it myself). Long before she was able to buy original art, she
decorated the house with rubbings from the friezes at Angkor. My high school friend Francis Coppola, who often sat
up with her after bringing me home from a date, learned
about Angkor Wat from her and, years later, used it for the
central scenes in his film *Apocalypse Now*.

Rita's amazing collections were masterpieces of eclecti-
cism and plenitude. She believed that if you could tell the
color of a wall in a room, you had failed in your interior
decoration, just as, if you could see the dirt in a garden, you
had failed as a gardener. But above all, she was interested

in everything modern, everything that thumbed its nose, preferably with irony, at the old-fashioned canons. So she collected Picasso and Juan Gris, but especially the Dadaists and surrealists, Marcel Duchamp, Max Ernst, and the German expressionist Georg Grosz.

Tales (and Sayings) from the Vienna Woods

Rita's tastes had been formed in Vienna, and her Viennese world came to me primarily in the form of German (or Viennese) sayings that she produced on various appropriate occasions and that still pop into my head on those, and often less appropriate, occasions. Here are a few of them. (I've translated them into English doggerel, but even readers with no German are urged to look at the German originals; a lot of the charm and silliness of the sayings, like that of all doggerel, is carried by the tight rhyme schemes.)

Whenever, as a little child, I hurt myself, she would take me on her lap and rock me in rhythm to this song:

Heia heia Segen, drei Tage Regen;
drei Tage Sonnenschein, wird es wieder gut sein.

There, there, bless you, three days' rain;
three days' sunshine, and you'll be well again.

In happier moments, I was, again, set on her lap and bounced up and down to the tune of a rather grim Teutonic sentiment:

Huppe huppe Reiter,
wenn er fällt dann schreit er.
Fällt er in den Graben,
fressen ihn die Raben . . .
Fällt er in den Sumpf
mach der Reiter plumpf!

Bumpety bump, he rides,
and when he falls he cries.
If he falls in water,
that will be his slaughter.
If he falls on the ground,
his body will never be found.
If he falls in the slop,
the rider falls . . . Kerplop!

And at the end, her knees opened and I fell through, still suspended above the ground by her hands.

As I grew older, two-line poems were sometimes cited to make a point. Often they were scatological:

Attila der Hunnen König
frisst soviel und scheisst sowenig.

Attila, the Hunnish King
wolfs his food and never shits a thing.

Or, alternatively,

Attila the king of the Huns
wolfs his food and never gets the runs.

I was never entirely sure what the moral force of that one was, but it was usually cited when I was acting ill-tempered. There was one saying that acknowledged the rare occasion when I was able to tell Rita something she didn't claim to know already:

Man wird so alt wie eine Kuh
und lernt doch immer noch dazu.

You get as ancient as a cow
and still learn something new somehow.

To this was sometimes added,

Man wird zu bald alt und zu spät klug.

You get old too soon and smart too late.

The whole philosophy of Rita's acquisitive Viennese world seemed to me to be captured in this short poem:

Schöne Leute haben schöne Sachen;
Wenn sie sie nicht haben, lassen sie sich sie machen.

Beautiful people have beautiful stuff;
and if they don't, they get it soon enough.

This often justified the purchase of yet another artwork, roughly equivalent to King Lear's "Reason not the need." Even a short phrase could be fraught with meaning: *Aufge-stellte Mausdrek* (a mouse turd stood on end) could be applied to a trivial person who acted as if he were a big shot. This is a term that I find very useful in academia.

The Mausdrek epithet was a purely Viennese saying, not a broader German one, and indeed Rita used many other Viennese locutions, such as the useful and highly irregular verb *äussedl*, made from the preposition *aussen* (outdoors, outside) plus an umlaut and the ever-present Viennese diminutive ending "l," and meaning, "to take outside a little," or more precisely, to take a dog out briefly to let him pee, as in the command "äussedl das Hund" (take the dog outside to pee), or, often, "äussedl das Dachl" (take the little dachshund outside to pee). The diminutive "l" was also the pivot of a joke on the English hotel in Vienna named the Bristol, which the Viennese called the *Hotel zu kleine Brust* (hotel of the little breast, which would be *Brüstl* in Viennese). And about small breasts, Rita cited a saying of the Viennese, who tend to be flat-chested:

Ein Handvoll ist fein;
mehr is gemein.

Petite is neat;
more is just a teat.

Diminutives also played a part in the saying "Man geht nicht zum Schmiedl, man geht zum Schmied" (You don't go to the smith-lette, you go to the smith), which is only roughly approximated by the English saying "Don't send a boy on a man's errand" (which she also said). Another Viennese-Bavarian expression, said when someone was, in her opinion, overly concerned with unimportant matters, was "Von was träumt die Gans? Von Kukkeretz!" (What does a goose dream about? Corn!). And a final Viennese favorite, "Wenn man dir gibt, nimm; wenn man dir nimmt, schrei" (When someone gives you something, take it; when someone takes something from you, yell), is a vivid expression of Viennese possessiveness and could have been on the Roth family coat of arms.

Other sayings were not particularly Viennese but more generally German: "Es ist noch nicht allertags abends" (It's not yet evening after the whole day), or, roughly, "It ain't over 'til the fat lady sings," said when I was relaxing too soon about something I hoped would happen. A related concept was "Man zeigt keinem Esel ein unfertiges Haus" (You don't show a donkey an unfinished house), said when I criticized something Rita was doing before it was completed. "Wem nicht zu raten, dem nicht zu hilfen" (Whom you cannot advise, you cannot help) was said *often* to me when I didn't do what she told me to do. This was often reinforced with "Gegen Dummheit kämpfen die Götter selbst vergebens" (Against stupidity even the gods fight in vain), a saying that I now find myself using just about every day. "Ein leerer Sack steht nicht" (An empty bag doesn't stand up) was said to me when I wanted to go off without breakfast.

There were many others: "Sie ist nicht auf dem Mund gefallen" (She never falls on her mouth) was said of someone who is never at a loss for words. "Frisches Gras / frisst der Haas" (Vegetables rare / are for a hare) betrayed Rita's scorn for salad. "Langes Fädchen / faules Mädchen" (Long thread / slugabed), which she sometimes translated into English as "Lazy man's load," was uttered when I tried to carry too many dishes at once. "Wie kommt der Kuhscheiss aufs Dach?" (How did cow shit get on the roof?) was generally used when someone asked her a stupid question that she couldn't or wouldn't answer. Sometimes this was followed by a bit of doggerel (or, perhaps, cowwerel):

Hat sich Kuh auf den Schwanz geschissen
und mit Schwung hinaufgeschmissen?

Did the cow shit on her tail
and then use it for a sail?

Some of these sayings turned out to be uncredited quotations from famous authors. This was the case with the much-invoked Latin phrase "Quod licet Jovi / non licet bovi" (pronounced in the Viennese manner, "Quod litset . . ."), or "What Jove may do / is not for you," literally, "What is permitted for Zeus is not permitted for a bull." This was the answer Rita gave whenever I claimed the right to do something because she did it. (It turns out that it comes from Eichendorf.) But she most often expressly quoted Goethe ("Also sagt Goethe" / Thus spake Goethe), usually from *Faust*. For example, "Die Bodeschaft höre ich wohl, jedoch mir fehlt der Glauben" (I certainly hear the news, but I lack belief), said by Faust when, on Easter morn, the people proclaimed, "Christ is risen," and said by Rita when I said something like "I practiced my Chopin nocturne today and didn't make any mistakes." She also frequently cited Goethe's aphorisms, of which the most puzzling was "Frisches ei, Gutes ei" (Fresh egg, good egg), a rather gnomic verse when applied to more abstract substances than eggs. (Rita always pronounced the initial "g" in words like *gnomic, gnostic,* and *gnu,* as she would have done in German — "gnädige Frau" — in part because she didn't want to waste the letter "g," as she explained.) And then there were the satires on Goethe quotes, of which my favorite was

> *Also sagt Goethe: der Arsch ist kein Flöte;*
> *Also sagt Schiller: ein Furz is kein Triller.*

> Thus spake Goethe: the ass is no flute;
> Thus spake Schiller, a fart is no toot.

This was spoken when someone broke wind.

Rita also had sayings in French: "Tant de bruit pour une omelette" (So much fuss for an omelette, or a tempest in a teapot) and English: "Coffee boiled is coffee spoiled." "Listen to men's words, but watch men's actions." "The road to Hell is paved with good intentions." "When Mozart was your age, he was dead." (I think she invented that one.) And she often quoted, as if they were German aphorisms, her favorite English authors, particularly Shakespeare ("The point envenomed too"). But she insisted that Shakespeare was really much better in German, in part because August Schlegel (who did the translation) was a better poet than Shakespeare, and in part because the German language was more musical than English. ("Sein oder nicht sein," she would intone, as evidence.)

From time to time, Rita would recite one of her favorite poems, by a lesser-known poet, Ferdinand Freiligrath, which Franz Liszt had set to music.[17] In particular, she cited the last lines when I said something angry and hurtful to her, as I fear I often did: "And guard your tongue well; a hard word quickly escapes. O God, I meant no harm by it, but the other went and wept."

The Oral Corpus of Rita Mythology

A body of tales (some, perhaps, apocryphal) about the crazy things that Rita had done circulated in the family during her lifetime and long after. Once, she put a toilet out in the backyard and said it was art, an *objet trouvé* just like those of Duchamp or Warhol. The neighbors complained to the board of health, and the board of health guy came and saw that the toilet wasn't connected, and went away. My brother Tony says that the neighbors claimed that Rita was preparing an outhouse for the thirty African children she was going to adopt, who weren't used to indoor plumbing. I do not know the source of that story and never heard it myself, but it sounds very much like something that Rita might do, or at least might say she would do, or that people might say she had said she would do, and I do remember the toilet.

On another occasion, objecting to the fact that many of our neighbors had, at the head of their front paths, black-faced jockeys holding lamps, she went out one night with her oil paints and painted all the jockeys' faces white. (This really did happen; I went with her that night, as lookout.)

Another much-told tale was one that I alone witnessed. We were driving in Manhattan and stopped at a light, but the automatic engine was racing a bit. A man suddenly stepped right in front of the car, startling Rita so that she took her foot off the brake; the car rolled forward a little, enough to knock him over; she put her foot back on the brake immediately, and he stood up in front of the car and started to curse her, using very strong language. She was so appalled and fascinated by his language that she took her foot off the brake again and the car rolled forward again and knocked him down again. This time he just picked himself up and walked away. He had an inkling of who he was up against.

Rita had a hysterectomy when I was about fifteen, Tony five. Lester brought us to visit her in the hospital when she was recuperating, and, apparently worrying about plummeting hormones and psychological reactions, he warned us that women after this sort of surgery often developed minor personality changes, and we should be particularly patient and understanding toward her. We edged nervously into Rita's hospital room, and there she was, sitting up in bed in her pink satin bed jacket, wearing a full red beard. Where she got it, or how she snuck it into the hospital, I never knew, but it certainly did break the ice.

Once when Rita came to visit me in England, I had just published a book, a Penguin Classic called *Hindu Myths*. As she walked down Malet Street to the University of London, where I was teaching, she passed Dillon's, the great bookstore, and saw in the window a display of Penguin books — but not mine. She went in and harassed the man until he added mine to the display, and then she continued on her way down Malet Street. When she told me what she had done, she remarked, "You know, all the other books were in the window only because the mothers of those authors put them there."

Many of her jokes were about death, the ultimate gallows joke. The punch line of one such joke played a key role in one of the many stories told about Rita and the opera. The occasion was March 4, 1960, when, near the end of Act II of *La Forza del Destino*, Leonard Warren sang the aria that begins, "Morir! Tremenda cosa!" (To die! A terrible thing!) and then "Urna fatale" (Fatal urn of my destiny!).

He finished the second aria, and then he keeled over. Rita, who knew the libretto well, realized immediately that he was not supposed to fall down at that point, that something was wrong, but most of the audience just assumed it was a bit of new stage business. The curtain rang down, and after some minutes, Rudolf Bing, the director of the Met at that time, stepped out and announced that Leonard Warren had died and that they would not continue the performance.[18] As the audience gasped with shock, Rita muttered, under her breath but still audible to those near her, "Give an enema!" Lester, horrified, hurried her out of the Met, and another Rita story entered the repertoire.

Now, Rita was simply referring to a highly relevant, though not particularly funny, old Jewish joke that turns upon the legendary Jewish reliance on the use of enemas for all internal problems. It went like this: An actor collapses onstage during a performance. Eminent doctors from the audience gather around him in the attempt to save his life. One old Jewish woman in the audience keeps shouting, "Give an enema!" Finally one of the doctors announces that the man is dead, but the woman keeps saying, "Give an enema!" In exasperation, the doctor turns angrily to the woman and says, "Madam, you don't understand; the man is *dead*," to which she replies, "Nu, so, it can't hurt."

So her remark was, one might say, true to the context, but not exactly in good taste . . . *Galgenhumor* had made its masterpiece.

CHAPTER FOUR

Who They Were to One Another

Great Neck

Rita and Lester met in Great Neck in the mid-1930s.

This town, on the North Shore of Long Island, was (in those days) a half-hour drive from Manhattan, or a half-hour ride on the Long Island Rail Road to Penn(sylvania) Station. Great Neck was easily *of* New York City, but not *in* it. For many years, Great Neck was one of the few towns on the North Shore where Jews could buy property; by that Gentleman's Agreement that Laura Hobson immortalized in her novel, and Gregory Peck in the film, most of the rest of the North Shore was "restricted." This meant that many of the talented and successful Jews who worked in Manhattan lived in Great Neck, including Broadway comedians (Eddie Cantor, Sid Caesar), opera singers (Richard Tucker), composers (Morton Gould), musicians (Leonard Rose, Leonid Hambro, Bobby Mann, Sascha Schneider, and practically the whole Budapest String Quartet), Hollywood moguls (Bob Benjamin of United Artists), and writers (Irving Stone).[19] In the film *The Women* (1939), the wealthy heroine, Norma Shearer, lives in Great Neck. In *Miracle on 34th Street* (1947), Santa

Claus lives in the Brooks Memorial Home for the Aged at 136 Maplewood Drive, Great Neck, and it is in Great Neck that little Nathalie Wood finds her dream house. There was a theater, the Playhouse, at which New York plays sometimes tried out.[20]

F. Scott Fitzgerald lived in Great Neck from 1922 to 1924 and wrote his best novel, *The Great Gatsby*, about Great Neck, which he called West Egg (where the Great [Neck] Gatsby lived). The unattainable Daisy lived in the next peninsula, East Egg, Manhasset. I've always thought that the secret of Gatsby was that he was Jewish: his past was shady, he was known to have changed his name, and his business partner (and the only person other than the narrator who attended Gatsby's funeral) was an unscrupulous and unsavory old Jew named Meyer Wolfsheim. When Gatsby gazed across Manhasset Bay at the green light that illuminated the dock of Daisy's house, she (the consummate shiksa) and it were unattainable because Jews could not buy property in Manhasset.

Great Neck had a famously good school system. My high school friends included Francis Coppola; Nobel Prize winner David Baltimore; Pulitzer Prize winner Steven Albert; Bernard Pomerance (author of *The Elephant Man*); and Bob Simon, the television correspondent who survived forty days in prison in Baghdad and then died in a car crash in Manhattan in 2015. Another member of my class was Barbara Stoler Miller, who, like me, earned a PhD in

Sanskrit in 1968, became a full professor, and was elected president of the Association of Asian Studies (she in 1990, I in 1998). What sort of odds would you give that the class of 1958 at Great Neck High School would yield two women who were, for quite a while, the only two American women Sanskritists with university chairs?[21] Something in the water? (Both of us married Great Neck boys, too.) But I am getting way ahead of my story.

How They Got Together in Great Neck

While Lester's family lived in Brooklyn, his older brother Jack had a pharmacy in Harlem, and Lester worked there; one of his jobs was selling condoms to prostitutes. In the late 1920s, Jack moved his pharmacy to Great Neck, and Lester would travel from Brooklyn to Great Neck to work for Jack in the Wychwood Pharmacy across from the Long Island Rail Road station. Lester told me that they left the cash register unlocked at night, because it was the most valuable thing in the store, and if a thief broke in, they didn't want him to smash the cash register. Eventually, Jack moved to Great Neck, and Lester often stayed with him there.

At that time, Rita's family lived in a big house on the main street in town, 179 Middle Neck Road, a few blocks from the Wychwood Pharmacy. But Lester and Rita didn't meet then, or there. They met, in the mid-1930s, on the public tennis courts off Fairview Avenue, in another part of Great Neck. Lester was waiting to meet a (male) friend for a game; Rita came onto the court and asked if he'd like to play. He refused, not wanting to waste time playing with a girl. But his friend didn't show up, and finally he felt it would be rude to refuse to play with her. Rita beat him thoroughly, in straight sets. She was a terrific tennis player, with an unreturnable serve, fast and low, just skimming the net. Indeed, sometimes it did not clear the net at all, and on those occasions most players used a safer second serve, slower and higher, to avoid double-faulting. But not Rita. If she faulted, her second serve was just as fast and low as the first, and often she double-faulted. She had no second serve. I wonder if Lester realized at that moment what that revealed about her personality — intense, risk-taking, talented, but above all totally uncompromising. If I wrote a book just about her, I would call it *No Second Serve*.

One thing led to another. After a while, Rita brought Lester home to meet her family. They married in 1938 and lived first in a small house in Little Neck, next to Great Neck (but farther from the water), and then, when I was about four years old, in another small house in Great Neck proper, on Tuddington Road. They played tennis doubles together for many years. She never did develop a safe second serve.

Minor Skirmishes

The tennis court was not the only place where Lester and Rita volleyed for the upper hand. On numerous occasions she played tricks on him, usually designed to teach him a lesson. For example:

Lester bought her a mink stole. All the rich matrons in Great Neck wore them, and she despised them. He kept pestering her to wear it, and finally he insisted (always a bad move with Rita) that she wear it to opening night at the Metropolitan Opera, which was, in those days, a very grand occasion. She met him there, dutifully wearing the mink stole, but wearing it over a bright orange iridescent sweat suit that she used to garden in.

He bought her a Jaguar. She didn't want a fancy foreign car, but he gave it to her anyway. She drove the Jaguar for a few days and then came home in a taxi, saying that the Jaguar had tried to kill her and she had abandoned it somewhere downtown. She went back to one of the small American economy cars that she favored.

There was a rule in our house that Lester was to leave business at the office; we did not entertain his business colleagues at home. But one day, a man from *Popular Science* was visiting from out of town, doing a publishing deal with Lester, and Lester asked Rita if he could bring the man home for dinner, to save him from dining alone in his hotel. She agreed, but Lester then went on to make a serious error of judgment: he asked her to prepare a better meal than usual, and to dress better than she usually did for a casual family dinner. Well, he brought the guy home, and Rita appeared wearing a dress fancier than her everyday costume, but on her head was my brother Tony's space helmet. She wore it throughout the dinner, opening the little door in front to put food into her mouth, but otherwise keeping it closed. She later argued that she thought it was appropriate for a man from *Popular Science*. Lester never again brought a business colleague home to dinner.

Isabeth Rosenberg Gross, a childhood friend of mine who knew Rita in those days, remembers a different, entirely mythologized variant of this incident, as she emailed to me in 2015: "Once when a repairman arrived, she answered the door wearing Tony's space helmet . . . and nothing else." One source of this variant of the story may well be the fact that, not on this occasion but quite often, Rita *did* appear stark naked around the house, unconcerned that she might be seen by neighbors or visitors. I have several photographs of her naked, one gazing out from the second story balcony of our summerhouse, another sitting meditatively on the floor of her bathroom. My brother Jerry was often embarrassed when his friends came upon her in the nude, and I myself remember several incidents of this sort, in which she shocked my friends. But not, as I recall, the man from *Popular Science*.

Money

HIS SPENDING

When they married, there was not enough money for a wedding ring. But when Lester made a lot of money, he had

Cartier make Rita a gold ring studded with diamonds and rubies, a kind of retrospective wedding ring. It was in the form of a "gimmal" ring, from the Latin *gemelli*, or twins: two rings joined together by a pivot so that when united, they constitute a single ring. There is a hand on each circlet, and when they are brought together, the hands clasp. Sometimes there is a third ring, with a heart, which appears when the hands are separated, and on which are usually inscribed the names of the lover and his beloved, "Antony to Cleopatra." This was the form of the ring my father gave my mother. But he had the heart inscribed "REF to SHU," her favorite volume of the eleventh edition of the *Encyclopædia Britannica* (1911), with its superb essays on Renaissance, Romanticism, Schiller, Schubert, Shakespeare, and so forth.

Lester loved using his money to live well. In 1953 we moved from Tuddington Road to a bigger house in Kenilworth, on King's Point, the tip of Great Neck and a much fancier part of town. We lived a few blocks from the water, and as we walked down to the dock, we passed the house of Paul Wittgenstein, the one-armed pianist for whom Ravel had written the concerto, and then the house of Sid Caesar.

Lester was famously generous, giving freely to causes and people he cared for. He always picked up the check. He liked to dine in good restaurants and to fly first class to good hotels in the Caribbean for winter vacations. He and Rita went to Paris and stayed at the Plaza Athénée, to Florence and stayed at the Four Seasons. He bought a graceful sailboat that he docked at the yacht club in Kenilworth; later, he bought a Chris-Craft that we sailed up the Hudson (Figure 7). (He attended an adult education course to learn navigation, and then he taught the course for several years.) We had a house in the Hamptons (Figure 25). Lester bought Rita a ten-seat box at the Metropolitan Opera for the entire season. He bought her, and me, expensive jewelry. He drove top-of-the-line Oldsmobiles, a new one every couple of years. (He drew the line at Cadillacs, which he regarded as ostentatious.)

His siblings said that Lester had "golden hands" (*geldene hende* in Yiddish), and indeed, he did seem to have the Midas touch. When we went to the Caribbean for vacations, while Rita was unpacking the suitcases, Lester sauntered down to the casino and returned in time for dinner, having won enough to pay for our entire vacation. He never went to a casino on any other occasion. (He played poker with a few friends, but only for pennies, which was a good thing, since he didn't have a poker face.)

After a while, Lester bought some horses, pacers, which he raced at Roosevelt Raceway and Yonkers Raceway. He called his stable Ganesha Stables, to please Rita, who collected statues of Ganesha. (He spelled the stable name in the technically more correct Sanskrit version, Ganesa [actually Gaṇeśa], to please me, as I was pedantic about Sanskrit in those days.) He bet only on his own horses, and they mostly lost, until there was one that was full of fire on the track and won a lot of races. I was sitting in the kitchen with Rita one summer afternoon when Lester came home from the track, his seersucker jacket folded over his arm. He was smiling a "cat that swallowed the canary" sort of smile as he came into the kitchen. Rita looked up and asked, "Did you win?" His answer was to reach for his billfold and peel off half a dozen $500 bills, saying, "That's your cut." Unfortunately, that horse was also so full of fire in the stable that he almost injured one of the grooms. Sadly, Lester sold him, despite his trainer's pleadings, and eventually sold the other horses too. But Ganesha Stable was wonderful fun while it lasted.

Years after Lester's death, on a visit to Rita, I saw that she still had a starting pistol from the old Ganesha Stable days; she kept *everything*. (It only fired blanks, and the barrel was leaded closed, but it sure *looked* like a pistol.) I asked to have it, and she said she would be glad to get rid of it; it made her nervous. I was flying back out of LaGuardia, with only hand luggage, so I suggested that I leave the gun there with her until some later visit, when I might put it in checked luggage, but she was insistent that I take it. Nervously, I set off for LaGuardia, planning to try to check it in some way, but I forgot, and only suddenly remembered it when I saw my carry-on bag moving relentlessly forward on the belt toward the X-ray. Horrified, I froze and watched it slide into the tunnel . . . and come out the other side, and nobody said a whispering word. So much for airport security. I use the pistol as a paperweight on my desk. From time to time it startles a visitor.

Recalling the early days when I often wanted a toy or game or doll like one that other children in school had and was told that we could not afford it, sometimes I asked Lester, "How much money do we have?" And he always answered, "Enough." The night before he went into what we all knew was likely to be a fatal surgery, he took great comfort in telling me how well he had provided for me and Tony and Jerry and Rita. And indeed, all through my life he had smoothed my road; all the years I was in school, he backed me so that I never had to work at anything but my studies. When I had a regular teaching job, I never had to teach in the summer to make ends meet. I could spend my summers writing. I was a Jewish princess. The money mattered.

HER ECONOMIZING

The money mattered to Rita, too, the money that paid for the big house and the box at the opera. But she and Lester fought all the time about money. Much, much later I wondered, in retrospect, if the money fights were a displacement for the fights they might have had, but didn't have, about other things — sex, religion, family, all the resentments and dissatisfactions that filled Rita, and perhaps Lester too, with frustration and suppressed fury. (Not pol-

1 In addition to Jack and Minnie Doniger (seated in the middle of the front row) and a number of their children and grandchildren, the main personae of my story are Simon (seated second from right) and, standing: Jerry and his wife Karren (third and fifth from left), Simon's wife Irma and daughter Ann (fifth and fourth from right), and Rita and Lester (third and second from right).

2 Lester as a little boy with his family in Russia, dated 1920. Lester is on the ground, on the left.

3 Lester and his sister Sonja in Raczki, circa 1920.

4 Lester and Ralph Raughley in front of the Book Club Guild building.

5 Lester and the Episcopal bishop.

6 Wendy on *Pulpit Digest*, May 1949.

7 Lester at the wheel of his Chris-Craft.

8 Lester in a formal photograph by Bachrach.

9 Lester near his death.

10 Lester sketched by Frank Kleinholz.

11 Hotel New York in Marienbad, now called the Polonia. Emil Baruch's initials appear below the fourth-floor balcony.

12 Copy of a painting depicting Elsa Baruch and Margaret (Gretl) Baruch as children, with their hoop, in front of the Colonnade in Marienbad.

13 Rita's father, Alex Roth.

14 Rita's mother,
Elsa Baruch Roth.

15 Rita with her nuclear family, circa 1945. From left: Juny's wife Taffy, Lester, Juny, Rita (in trousers), Grandpa Alex Roth, Dorothy, Harry, Jerry, Elsie, Grandma Elsa Roth, and Wendy in front.

16 Rita with her siblings and the older generation of her family, at the Czardas Restaurant. From left: Isabelle Singer (an old friend), Harry, Harry's wife Pam, Elsie's husband Mortie, Elsie, Lester, Hans, Hans and Lisl's daughter Daisy and her husband, Lisl, Gretl, Rita, Grandpa Alex Roth.

17 Rita as a little girl in Vienna, in front of the Hofburg, with an unknown woman, perhaps her governess.

18 Rita young, perhaps in Marienbad.

19 Rita, July 1934
(aged 23), in Great Neck,
with a dachshund.

20 Rita in the kitchen, circa 1970.

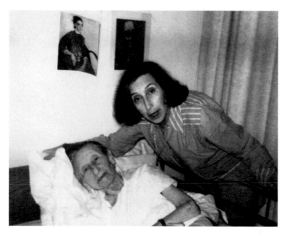

21 Rita at her mother's deathbed, 1980.

22 Rita's eightieth birthday, near her death, 1991.

23 Rita sketched by Frank Kleinholz.

24 Lester and Rita
with newborn Wendy,
1940.

25 Lester and Rita at the house in the Hamptons,
November 1970.

26 Lester with two unidentified women.

LESTER AND WENDY

27 Lester holding
Wendy as a baby, 1940.

28 Lester and Wendy.

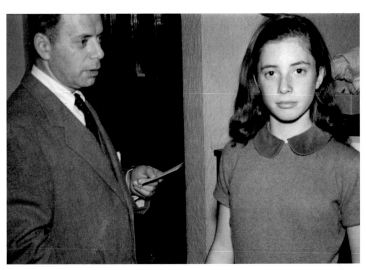

29 Lester and Wendy.

LESTER AND TONY

30 Lester and Rita with Tony.

RITA AND WENDY

31 Rita with Wendy,
circa 1948.

32 Rita with Wendy in India, 1964.

33 Rita with Wendy in Oxford, 1973.

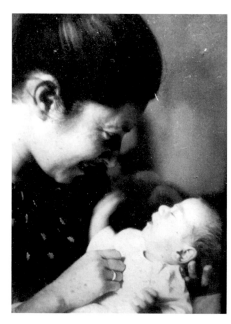

34 Wendy with newborn Michael, 1971. Photo kept on Rita's bedside.

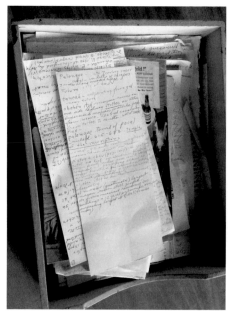

35 A box of Rita's notes.

itics, because when they fought about politics they *did* fight, bitterly, about politics.) But their fights about money were certainly (also) fought about money. The fable of the grasshopper and the ants always reminded me of that ongoing warfare of theirs.

Though Rita inhabited Lester's world of expensive vacations and racehorses, she carved out within it another economic planet, a sphere of watchful parsimony. The trauma of losing everything they had had in Vienna was compounded in Rita by something quite different, a hatred of waste, which was based in part on her European upbringing (Europeans, having suffered through two world wars, were always appalled by American wastefulness) and in part on her Communist respect for labor. "Think of all the work that went into growing that wheat, and harvesting it, and baking the loaf," she would say to me when I was about to throw away a piece of bread. But it was also based in part on a sense of ecology that was decades ahead of its time. "Waste not, want not" was her mantra. She couldn't even bear to waste space. Whenever she put away leftover food, she would take great pains to fit the food into the exact-sized container that would hold it all and that it would fill entirely. When Lester went on business trips, she would pack his suitcase so that every single thing fit in and it could *just* close. Even if he did not buy anything on the trip (and he usually did), he could not possibly repack the suitcase as well as she had packed it, so he always ended up having to buy another suitcase to get everything home. Our attic was full of the suitcases he'd bought on those trips. The attic also had a big, walk-in cedar closet, always locked, in which Rita kept presents that she bought whenever she found something that struck her fancy and was a bargain. She saved them up until Christmas or a birthday came around, and then chose out of her store just the right present for the person whose occasion it was. Once she bought a half-dozen shoes in different sizes and colors — lime green, hot pink, orange — because they were a terrific bargain, and she offered them to people whose feet, she hoped, might be the right size.

Rita's passion for saving time and space as well as money made her take pride in finding ways to drive from Great Neck to Manhattan in record time, without paying tolls at either the 39th Street (Queens Midtown) tunnel or the Triborough Bridge. Her route involved elaborate twists and turns through the industrial area of Queens, until, at a crucial moment, you smelled the bread from a nearby factory and turned onto a side ramp to the 59th Street (Queensboro) Bridge. "Turn left when you smell the bread" was her instruction, and it always worked. (Similarly, she told me when to turn off Northern Boulevard to get from Great Neck to LaGuardia: "Get off when you smell the low tide.") I always think of her when I smell the cool skunky smell of a low tide, or the warm velvety smell of bread from a factory.

Our house was always cold and dark, as Rita went about turning out lights and turning down thermostats, in part to lower household bills but also because it was sinful to waste energy. In the old house when I was little, my room was always icy cold. There were no curtains on the windows, for Rita felt they trapped the heat. Right outside my bedroom window was a tree whose bare branches would scrape against the window at night with a squeaking sound like chalk on a blackboard. Sometimes, when the tree was coated with ice, a nearby street lamp would light up the glassy branches so that they shimmered and glowed as if from within. The thermostat was always turned way down at night and set to come back on just a half hour before we got up in the mornings. When I went up to bed, I'd take the dachshund up with me, and I'd lift the covers and she'd jump onto the bed and burrow right down under the sheets to the bottom, so that by the time I got undressed and into my pajamas and climbed into the bed, it was all cozy and warm under the blankets. (To this day, I find a warm dog—nowadays a golden retriever—the perfect bed warmer.)

Rita economized everywhere. Outgrown clothes could be stretched another year or two by opening seams and/ or stitching in inset strips. Everything was recycled, long before there was even a word for it. We never bought wax paper or aluminum foil; Rita saved the wrappings from loaves of bread and the inside layer of cereal boxes, imparting the incompatible flavors of Kellogg's corn flakes and Special K to the sandwiches she wrapped for us for school. She never threw anything out. After her hysterectomy, she used her old diaphragms to cover jelly jars. It was one of my secret pleasures to watch the faces of guests served from one of those jars as they puzzled over the object they could not quite place, and then the sudden wide-eyed stare as they figured it out.

Rita had collections of egg cartons and bottles and jars and paper bags and string and newspaper and cardboard boxes and plastic boxes and plastic bags and paper clips and the plastic spoons and forks you get with take-out and a thousand things I cannot recall. She saved the paper that presents came wrapped in, and insisted that we, too, unwrap our presents without tearing the paper (an agonizing task for an impatient young child at Christmas or birthday). She later used that paper to wrap presents for other people. Determined to foil her, Ralph Raughley brought her a present wrapped in heavy, expensive paper that had "Happy Birthday" printed on it over and over again; he had then written "Rita" under every "Happy Birthday" in red ink to keep her from using it again. Not to be outdone, she carefully saved the paper, and then, when the time came for Ralph's birthday, she wrapped his present in the same paper, simply writing "from" before every "Rita," in red ink.

When she was doing all this, she was so far ahead of her time that she seemed madly eccentric. In her politics and her artistic tastes, she knew she was part of a larger move-ment, an avant-garde. But in what we would now call her environmentalism, she not only had no allies but had no categories in which to explain to herself, let alone to any-one else, why she was doing what she was doing. She was all the way out there alone, an avant-garde of one.

Lester, who liked to buy the best, stocked the open bar in the downstairs hall with the finest brands of the day, Chi-vas Regal and Courvoisier and Tanqueray and so forth. But when a bottle was emptied, Rita would refill it with a cheap brand, in part to save money, in part to put a spoke in Les-ter's wheel, and in part to prove that people didn't notice what they tasted but simply responded to brand names. I used to love to sit on the stairs, which gave me a good view of the hall and the bar, and watch a guest stroll over, raise his eyebrows approvingly at the posh labels, pour out a glass from one of them, and take a sip — only to recoil with a grimace, a frown, and a second look at the label. I was shopping for liquor with Rita once when she asked the salesman for his most inexpensive cooking sherry. "You know, madam," he replied, "you and your guests will taste the quality of the sherry even when it is cooked. You really should cook with a sherry as good as the sherry that you drink." "I drink cooking sherry," she replied, and that was the end of that. After we had had a dinner party, Rita would collect all the wine glasses and brandy glasses and pour whatever was left in them onto a fruit cake that she kept for that purpose and served on New Year's Eve, by which time it must have been about 1,000 proof.

Over the years, Rita managed to save enough money from what Lester gave her for housekeeping to establish a sizeable secret nest egg. She used a lot of it to buy artworks, inexpensive things at the start, more important works later on. She was so fiercely independent and defiant that she wouldn't ask Lester for money he would gladly have given her. She always made sure that what she bought was a bargain, and she was always right. She had a superb eye and carefully researched the art that interested her and all the auctions that had sold an artist's work, as a tout would consult the racing form before betting on a horse. She bought a Stuart Davis for $750, a Corot, a Marsden Hartley, a Gabriele Muenter, all somehow magically transmuted from lowered thermostats and recycled wax paper.

After a while, Rita had so much cash stashed away that she worried about losing it and established a bank account all her own (also amassing *ein bissel* interest) that she told no one about. (As a mere housewife, she filed no separate return and had not mentioned her account to Lester.) But there is a telling entry in one of her notes: "Ask Brody [Nat Brody, Lester's tax accountant] if a wife has no source of income other than her husband. Can *anything* purchased during the course of marriage be said to be *hers*? Or how is *her* possession and ownership of anything established? She buys an object which accrues in value — her husband

dies — has she 'inherited' it? Or was it hers? How *does* she
establish ownership and possession?" Alas, the bank naturally told the IRS about Rita's secret account, and the IRS
therefore subjected Lester to an extensive, and expensive,
audit. They had a terrific fight about that.

One of the most serious fights that I remember was
about the body and soul of books. Among Rita's many
wonderful collections, her first editions were particularly
wonderful. She bought first editions only of books that
she loved, and only of books that were worth a lot more
than she paid for them, but she never let anyone read them.
They were valuable, and their value might be diminished if
they were actually read, perhaps damaged. Her reverence
for first editions infuriated me. I liked a paperback that I
could drop into a bathtub, throw into a backpack, spill tea
on, *use*. Lester, who as a publisher knew full well that the
actual physical value of a book, its paper and ink and glue,
was only a matter of pennies (all the rest coming from the
human hours put into its writing and production and mar-
keting), shared my view. On the trip that we took together
to Marienbad in 1958, he brought along a copy of the Modern Library edition of *War and Peace*, a book that he had
reread many times. But as it was a very big book, and he
liked to have it with him to read as the spirit moved him, he
tore it into about eight or ten pieces, and carried with him
each day just the bit he was reading at the moment. Rita regarded this as mayhem, the waste of a precious artifact, an

insult to the author, an unforgivable act of desecration, the loss of value. She didn't talk to him for days and days.

Food

It was in the realm of food that Rita's obsessions about frugality and saving exercised their greatest power. Leftover food that could not be re-used in a stew or a soup (she offered a prize to anyone who could identify all the ingredients in one of her soups, and it was never claimed) was put into our compost heap. She saved leftover coffee to make into coffee ice cubes for iced coffee. Long before restaurants supplied doggie bags, Rita would ask the waiter to give the leftovers to us for our dog. Once, but only once, when I was very young (and we did not have a dog), I exclaimed, "But Mommy, we don't have a dog."

Rita was a terrific cook when she could be persuaded to use the right ingredients (Figure 20). One of her specialties was Palatschinken, a kind of paper-thin, almost transparent Czech crepe that she made in a special pan that resembled a wok with steep sides, which she had brought over from Vienna. She would make the special batter and let it sit for a while, then heat a little oil in the pan and, when it was very hot, pour in just a spoonful of the batter, swishing it about the moment it hit the pan so that it coated the pan right up to the top rim. Then "Hup!" she would toss it up in the air so that it flipped over and landed right in the pan. Another "Hup!" and it slid right onto your plate. The whole operation took just the amount of time it has taken me to describe it. You spread apricot jam on it, rolled it up, picked up the tube and ate it from the end, like a candy cane. She made Palatschinken as a special treat whenever one of us came home from college and on other special occasions. She could make a fabulous Linzer torte too, spending the whole day roasting the hazelnuts in the oven and laboriously peeling and crushing them.

But the day-to-day meals were treacherous. When she shopped for food, Rita bought the fruit and vegetables that had been "reduced for quick sale," past their prime or damaged. She bought meat that the butcher sold off cheaply at the end of the day. She kept food for weeks and weeks, until green mold was visible; when we complained, she retorted, "What do you think penicillin is made of?" The results, though cooked with skill, were generally inedible. When my brother Tony was small, he went to play at a friend's house for the first time, and when he came back, he eagerly told us the amazing thing he had seen: "They have *new food!*" I loved the food at Radcliffe College, and the food on airplanes, because I knew it wasn't made from leftovers. It was new food.

Lester, having lunched with colleagues in Manhattan at the 21 Club or the Forum of the Twelve Caesars or Lutèce, took one or two symbolic bites at dinner and blamed his lack of appetite on his heavy lunch. The rest of us thought of some excuse (mustard, another glass of water) to send

Rita back into the kitchen. While she was out of the room, we chattered away loudly while we lowered our plates silently below the table, where the dachshund licked them almost clean before we replaced them on the table and ate the last bits ourselves in front of her.

For the rule was that we couldn't leave the table until we had eaten everything on our plates. When I was a child in a high chair, I was a very slow eater, a dawdler. On at least one occasion, breakfast went on until lunch, at which time the unfinished breakfast plate was removed and the lunch plate placed on the high chair tray; then lunch went on to dinner, and eventually I was taken down from the high chair to go to bed. We were required to clean our plates even in restaurants. Rita had a German saying for this:

Lieber den Magen sich verrenken
als dem Wirt etwas zu schenken.

Sooner make your stomach break
than let the waiter take your steak.

My older brother Jerry says he was well into high school before he learned that the Clean Plate Club was not a national institution. My little brother Tony, however, the one who became a lawyer, was not so gullible, even as a young child. When Rita insisted that the poor starving children in China would be glad to have the food he refused to eat, he replied, "Name three." Years later, when I read

Jung Chang's *Wild Swans: Three Daughters of China* (1991), I learned that Chinese mothers, urging their children to eat scavenged roots and mushrooms in a time of widespread starvation, would say to them, "The starving children in America would be glad to have it." Clearly this was an international conspiracy.

Sex

Women found Lester attractive (Figure 26). The stripper Faith Dane,[22] who was a friend of the family (introduced by Lee Hambro), invariably made a pass at Lester when she came to the house. We wondered if he had a mistress, a figure whose existence we had reason to suspect, but without hard evidence. He kept an apartment in Manhattan, in Tudor City (on East 40th Street and FDR Drive), allegedly in order to be able to shower and change after business and before the opera, but it may well have had other uses. Some of my high school girlfriends had crushes on him, and some years later, he invited one of them out on several occasions. In the summer of 1958, when Rita and Lester and I were in Vienna, I went with Lester to a store on the Ringstrasse, where he bought three pieces of jewelry; at Christmas, he gave one to my mother and another to me, but the third one had vanished, and I wondered if he had given it to a mistress. Long after Lester's death, Rita once remarked of him, "All the women were crazy about him and I was hoping that he'd get a mistress, but he didn't, of course. He was incapable." This was recorded in our NPR interview in 1990. At this cryptic moment, I interrupted her nervously ("Tell him about Daddy and *Pulpit Digest*," I begged), so I never did find out precisely what it was that she regarded Lester as incapable of, sex or infidelity.

Her hope was based in large part on her own dislike of sex. She couldn't understand why I kept falling in love and/ or into bed. She didn't like the hairiness of men. She told me, long after Lester's death, that she didn't like sleeping with him. Early in their marriage, she charged him a quarter (Tony thinks it was probably a nickel) for every time they did it, and saved up the nickels (or quarters) in a glass jar; she used them, together with the money siphoned off from her household allowance, to buy artworks. They had separate, single beds in the same room, with the bed table between them. (He thrashed about all night, and the covers were in a terrible mess by morning; she slept absolutely still, the covers smooth in the morning.) When she was up all night downstairs, she was not upstairs in bed with Lester. And I've come to think that this was no accident.

Rita told me that in Vienna, in the 1920s, she had been in love with an older man, a publisher (!). Her father had broken it up. She said that this man in Vienna was the only man she had ever loved, that she had never loved Lester, and that she had married him to get away from her father. Yet (she continued) she knew Lester was a good man, and she never left him. She strongly implied that she had stayed with him for my sake and Tony's, because she found her happiness in us. I also thought, though she did not say this, that she may have stayed because she did not want to replicate the destruction wrought by her mother's bolting. There is an extraordinary entry about love in her notes: "Love can best be likened to litigation. Being loved is like being sued. One has had it, and one is done for once the act is initiated. Whether the stone hits the jug, or the jug hits the stone, it's bad for the jug. Even if one wins, the cost of the action must be borne. One is involved by the action of the aggressor no matter how passive one is or has been. To be addressed or faced is an involvement; to be an object is enough."

And there is, elsewhere in her notes, a strange, rather cryptic, fragmentary stanza:

Think rather that I am cold
that all I know of loving　·
is what I have been told.

Rita was fascinated by lesbians and gay men. Lillian Hellman and Gertrude Stein were her great heroes, and she always insisted that half the leading men in Hollywood, particularly John Wayne (whose real name, she would point out, mockingly, was Marion!), were gay. She once remarked that Burt Lancaster fucked anything that moved, male or female. She had many openly gay male friends, including her oldest friend, Graham Singer, though I never knew her to have a gay female friend. There is a passage about this in her notes, too:

> natural homo tendencies suppressed by guilt and brainwashed image of acceptable he-she behavior. aberration vilified and family idealized. urge of male for female not science but social and clerical ideal. man isn't an animal dominated by sex urge to reproduce but *reasons* and when unbrainwashed thinks for himself. homosexuals *are* smarter, clearer, creative. they are the ones freed from brainwashing and imposed criteria of behavior. they are per se more creative and freer spirits. less inhibited less suppressed. most frequent and interesting and important response is anger and indignation which meets observations that someone is gay. ergo gay is bad and pejorative and unacceptable.

During our NPR interview in 1990, Rita insisted that Jesus was gay. She said, "I'm quite sure that Christ was a homosexual. There's no question in my mind. But nobody would say that. It's indecent. It would never be mentioned. It was simply mentioned that he was holy." When I asked, "How do you know Jesus was homosexual?" she replied, "Well, he had all these women who were crazy about him, and he never touched a woman in his life. That was later on regarded as a holy thing. But that's nonsense. He was a brilliant man. He was just never interested in fucking women and he never did. But that's natural to me. I don't think what's expected of men is a natural, normal thing. Because men and women are no different from animals. Of course a lot of them are not interested in the other sex. And I don't think that's bad, or indecent, or anything. I think it's a very natural thing." On another occasion, she gave more arguments: Jesus never married; all his friends (the Apostles) were gay; and (this was the clincher) you could see that he was gay just by looking at him. ("How?" I asked). In all the paintings, of course.

His Death in Russia and Great Neck, 1971

One day in the late 1960s, staying at a fancy hotel in London, where the bathroom was made entirely of mirrors, Lester had noticed for the first time a lump on the inside of his thigh. He flew home and was soon diagnosed with cancer. Surgery removed the lump, and he seemed to be okay, at least for a while. I was due to go to Moscow with my husband, a historian of Russia, so we left for an academic year (1970–71). (I had finished my Harvard PhD dissertation in 1968 and would spend our year in Russia turning it into a book.) In Moscow, my closest friend was Tasya Elizarenkova, a great Sanskritist who was defiantly dedicated to the Russian Orthodox Church, a dangerous thing to be in those Cold War days of Communism under Brezhnev, whose reign vehemently persecuted all religions. When Tasya learned how Lester loved Tolstoy, she went with me to Yasnaya Polyana, Tolstoy's home and grave. There I gathered some leaves from the forestland around the grave to bring home to Lester.

One day in April 1971, I was called to the communal phone in our dorm at Moscow State University out in Lenin Hills; it was Rita. Despite the poor connection, I heard her say that the cancer had returned, and they were going to do some further surgery, but not cut off his leg. "Of course they're not going to cut off his leg!" I shouted. "You didn't hear me," she replied. "I said, they are going to cut off his leg." My husband and I flew back and went straight to the hospital. I gave Lester the leaves from Yasnaya Polyana. He was very happy to learn that I was pregnant. (When Michael was born, we gave him the middle name of Lester.) We said our goodbyes (Figure 9). After the surgery, which was more radical than first planned (it was a hemi-pelvectomy), Lester fell into a coma from which he never emerged. After several days of waiting and hoping, my visa was up and I had to return to Moscow. On April 27, I received a call from the American ambassador in Moscow, who told me that Lester had died. I called Rita, who said that, as there was to be no ceremony, I should stay in Moscow; she was having him cremated, and that was that. It felt wrong not to do anything about my father's death, to go on without any closure, as if nothing had happened, but what could I do?

I was to meet Tasya for lunch that day and could not reach her to cancel; she had no phone. I met her and told her what had happened, and how unreal and disconnected I felt. "Your father was born in Russia, wasn't he?" she asked. "Come with me." Tasya then took me on a long journey across Moscow, first by subway, then a walk, then a tram, and then another walk. We ended up at a small, plain, three-story apartment house. Tasya knocked at the door, and a woman appeared; there were words, the woman angry, looking at me, Tasya insistent and conciliatory. Finally we were admitted. We walked through a hall, a kitchen (people seated at the table looked up as we passed), a sitting room, another hall, until we entered a dark, windowless room that smelled of incense. From a door in the opposite wall a man entered, fastening and adjusting the robes of a Russian Orthodox priest. We were in an underground church. "You must never tell anyone where this is," whispered Tasya. I promised, and indeed I could not have found it again if I had tried. Tasya said, "Your father was born here; here is where he will end." She told the priest my father's name (Eleazar Doniger) but did not mention that he was Jewish, and the priest performed the ceremony. They would not let me give them money. Tasya and I left, and I went back to my room in Lenin Hills, and to the rest of my life. It seemed strangely appropriate that Lester, who had spent so much of his life working with Christians, should have his soul laid to rest by one of them (albeit Russian Orthodox, a very different stripe from American Protestants) instead of one of his own people, American Jews. Yet the Russians were his own people, too.

Her Death in Great Neck, 1991

But I felt bad that nothing had been done with his ashes. When I finally came home from Moscow, as I hung up my coat, I saw a box on the shelf in the coat closet. "That's Daddy," said Rita. The obituary in the *New York Times* had said, "Funeral service will be private." It was certainly private: a box in a closet.

Twenty years passed. Rita continued to live in the big house in Great Neck. Her sisters urged her to sell it and move to an apartment in the city, as all their aging friends were doing, instead of "rattling around" in all the big rooms. "I don't *rattle*," she said. "I walk from room to room, looking at my paintings." And for a while, she continued to go to Manhattan to the opera and concerts and auctions and new exhibits at MOMA and the Guggenheim and the Metropolitan Museum. But after about ten years, she stopped going out, and for the final five years of her life, she spent most of her time in bed, sleeping or watching reruns of her beloved *Kojak* and *Columbo* and *Rockford Files*. On August 8, 1991, she died, alone, suddenly, quietly. She was eighty (Figure 22).

Though Rita had, again, requested that there be no ceremony, I had had enough of that. I insisted that we bury *both* of them, properly. Because they had been cremated, it was not easy to find a Jewish cemetery that would bury them, but when the director of the big Jewish cemetery near us learned that it was Lester who was being buried, he expressed shock and concern that twenty years had passed in this way, for he knew Lester as a pillar of the Jewish community, and he bent the rules so that the ashes of both of our parents could be buried there.

It was, after all, primarily Rita's funeral; hers was the recent death. But on the day, a rainy day just like funerals in the movies, none of Rita's siblings showed up at the cemetery—conflicted about her to the very end. (Later they said they had mixed up the time.) As my brothers and I stood there with the rabbi, one by one cars appeared, every single one of Lester's relatives within driving distance (there were quite a few). One had learned about this occasion and told the others, and they came, all of them greatly relieved to end the distress that they had lived in for the twenty years during which Lester was never officially mourned. And that is how Lester, appropriately, had two funerals, one Christian and one Jewish.

(Rita, too, had two funerals, and the first had also been a Christian funeral. For some months had passed between her death and the ceremony in which we buried both of their ashes. Before that, I had felt the need for some sort of ritual, as I had felt for Lester twenty years earlier. I called on my dear friend David Tracy, a Catholic priest who taught with me, in the Divinity School at the University of Chicago [and who was actually on the board of *Pastoral Psychology*, I later learned]. Father Tracy agreed to say a Latin mass for Rita, in the lovely Irish chapel hidden away in one of the theological schools in Hyde Park. All my friends who had known her came to the service; we felt that she would have appreciated the Latin, and in deference to her, we omitted the Eucharist. Then we all went back to my house and told one another our stories about her.)

On the day of the joint funeral, Rita's sisters, who had failed to make it to the burial, swarmed into our house afterwards, carrying plates full of things they had baked. They took over the kitchen and the dining room, exchanging compliments and recipes. No one said a word about Rita. I grew angrier and angrier, and finally I went over to the stereo system and put on the tape that Rita had made with me for the NPR interview in 1990. I turned up the volume, and the sound of Rita's voice boomed into all the rooms of the house. Her sisters froze with their forks halfway to their mouths, as Rita confided in the interviewer, "My sisters believe things, they go by rules, for no reason at all, just since everybody says it and it's written down, so that's it. And I say, well, think about it!" I was pleased to let her have the last word at her own wake.

But in fact it was my son Mike who had already had the last word about Rita. Shortly after she died (before the ceremony in Chicago and many months before we held the burial and the gathering of her siblings in the house), I had gone with Mike to meet Tony in the house in Great Neck. (Rita had left a specific bequest to Jerry, with the rest to be shared between Tony and me.) We divided up the books and paintings by flipping a coin for who went first, and then taking turns choosing our favorite paintings, and leaving the rest to be sold at auction. When it came to the first editions, there were so many that we began by dividing them into halves (A to M and N to Z), and then we picked out our favorites and traded them like baseball cards: "I'll give you my Dickens for your Gertrude Stein," "My Lewis Carroll for your Shakespeare," and so forth. We left everything else in the house.

We loaded up our U-Hauls and drove away, Tony up the coast to Boston, Mike and I west to Chicago. But before we could get out of the driveway, Hurricane Bob struck —it was August 1991. Bob chased Tony up the coast and chased Mike and me over the Throgs Neck Bridge, which was swinging back and forth like a hammock as we inched over it. We got through and drove to Cleveland, where we stayed overnight in a hotel. Upstairs in our room, we turned on the television for news of the hurricane and saw Yeltsin standing on a tank, in the aftermath of a failed coup against Gorbachev that meant the beginning of the end of the Soviet Union.

"Well," said I, "it's a good thing grandma didn't live to see this."

"No," replied Mike, "they didn't dare do it as long as grandma was alive."

CHAPTER FIVE

Who They Were to Me

Rita and Lester were born into a world of chaos, in Russia and Vienna, the war, the pogroms, the Holocaust. They had come to America from Europe searching, like modern pilgrims, for freedom *from* religion. In America, they worked hard and made sacrifices, to build a secure, protected childhood for their children. They gave us the safety they had never had. They gave us the chance to become what they could not become, or what they wanted us to become, or what we wanted to become.

How My Brothers and I Had Different Parents

I am an only child with two brothers. That is, I grew up with all the advantages and disadvantages of an only child, since my brothers were separated from me by a vital decade on each side, but now I have two brothers whom I cherish. My brothers and I have *very* different views of our parents, a fact that has multiple explanations. Each of us lived our first decade in an entirely different time period: my older brother, Jerry, the 1930s, myself the 1940s, and my younger brother, Tony, the 1950s. Just as there were twenty years between Lester and Jack (and twenty years between my parents' deaths), there were twenty years between Tony and Jerry. The whole planet changed in major ways during those decades.

But there is a simpler and more specific explanation for why each of us mythologized Rita and Lester so differently: we are mythologizing entirely different people. My older brother Jerry actually *was* the child of different parents — his mother was Lester's sister Katy, and his father a man who disappeared from the scene before I ever entered it. Lester always regarded Jerry as his son, but Rita resented having to take care of him in the very first year of her marriage, when she was finally free of her father, and she did not always treat Jerry well. When she became bedridden near the end of her life, of the three of us, Jerry was the one who visited her most often, and when she was dying, she apologized to him for not treating him well when he was young. He said, with his characteristic generosity, "Nonsense, you and Lester did everything for me; I have nothing but gratitude for you." And so that ended well. But because Jerry's first decade was not spent with the two people who ultimately raised all three of us, I will here concentrate on the contrast between Tony and me.

In the decade between the moment of my birth and Tony's, 1940 to 1950, everything had changed. When I was born (Figure 24), we were not rich, and Rita cared for me largely by herself. Lester worked long hours at the office; I saw him mostly on weekends and vacations. When Tony was born, we were rich. We had a maid, an African American woman who lived in "the maid's room" and wore a uniform (and should have been, it now seems to me, much more of an embarrassment for Jewish liberals than she was). After school, I would often go back to "the maid's room" and watch soap operas with her on her television set as she ironed (*Love of Life*, *As the World Turns*). Since Rita now stayed in bed most of the day and stayed up most of the night, the maid prepared breakfast for Tony and me, and Lester presided over it. Lester's business was now well established, and he could spend more time at home.

Moreover, the fact that Tony was a son and I a daughter made a great difference to both parents. To Lester, it meant Little League and Boy Scouts and trout fishing trips (and Hebrew lessons), and so I always felt that he was a far more present presence to his son than he had been to his daughter. Rita, being a passionate feminist, *avant la lettre*, wanted to make sure that her daughter would accomplish all the things that she herself had never had a chance to do, so she kept after me night and day, whereas, when Tony came along, she loved him dearly but did not try to make him into anything. Lester raised Tony and formed his personality: easygoing, cheerful, gregarious, happily married, reliable, consistent, conventional, fit, tactful — in a word, Apollonian. And Rita raised me, forming my personality: driven, high-spirited, a loner, divorced, rebellious, unpredictable, a maverick, fat, outspoken — in a word, Dionysian.

But when I mentioned this distribution of the parental alliances and influences to Tony, he replied that, on the contrary, he had always felt that he knew Rita better than he knew Lester, in part because he knew her for twenty years longer than he knew Lester, but also because, as he put it in a 2015 email, Rita "wore her personality on her sleeve while Lester's was under cover. Because she was much more emotional than he was there was a deeper (not necessarily pleasant, at times) connection with her than with him." Moreover, where I found Rita fiercely controlling, someone to be resisted, Tony found her benignly neglectful, someone to learn from. She interacted with him in a much more casual way, teaching him, for instance, to cook and garden, which he does very well but I resolutely refused to learn. Then, too, I was the older child, who had to earn the love of her parents, while Tony was the younger, the Benjamin, beloved just by the simple fact of his existence. The fact that Rita had Tony when I was growing up and drifting away from her may have made him all the dearer to her. And indeed, Tony married a woman very much like Rita in temperament, famously high-spirited and strong-minded. When he first met her father and declared his intentions, his future father-in-law warned him about what he was taking on, to which Tony replied, "Have you met my mother?"

Both of us adored Lester, but again in different ways. Since I knew him for ten years longer than Tony did, Lester was there for me when I married and divorced and married again (though he was long gone by the time of the second divorce), while his death at sixty-one meant that Tony's wife never met Lester. And I knew more about Lester's childhood than Tony did; Tony can't recall a single discussion with him about his pre-America past, and always felt or assumed that he did not want to talk about it and wanted to forget about it. But he and Tony were guys together, and Tony knew far more than I did about Lester's publishing business. Each of us envied the other for knowing Lester better.

My Relationship with Lester

We used to say that Rita was the funny bunny, Lester was the money bunny, Tony was the sunny bunny, and I was (to Lester) the honey bunny.

One of my favorite stories about Lester involves a red velvet dress that I inherited when I was four or five years old from the child of a wealthier friend. It was too big at first, but Rita took it in; after a while it was too small, and she let it out, and later she added lace borders on the sleeves and hem to stretch it still further. I never wore it out because I wore it only on special occasions and was careful not to damage it. But I finally outgrew it. Even Rita had to admit defeat, and we gave it away. Fast-forward twenty-five years: I am going to an elegant New Year's Eve party in Manhattan, and Rita takes me to Henri Bendel to buy me, on sale, a fabulous dress, a Bill Blass original, made of red velvet, cut daringly on the bias, with an asymmetrical plunging neckline and a plunging back too. I put on the dress; my hair is piled high in an elegant chignon; I have borrowed some of Rita's best jewelry. I go downstairs to where Lester is reading the newspaper. "Daddy, look at me!" He looks up and smiles and says, "You still have that red velvet dress."

I was Daddy's little girl, and he was the parent I loved best. He always approved of everything I did; he thought I was wonderful. When I was young, I didn't see him much during the week, but Saturday mornings he spent with me. Sometimes we would walk to a wooded area near our house, where there was a stream with a natural clay bed; we used to scoop up the clay and I would later work with it at home. But usually on Saturdays I went to the office with him (his office building was in Great Neck, a few miles from where we lived), and I played with the mimeograph machines while he checked stuff. Sometimes we visited the printer in his shop, a magical place, like a toymaker's den. On one occasion, when I was in kindergarten, I became so angry with Rita (I cannot now recall the specific *casus belli*, there were so many possibilities) that instead of walking home from school (ah, those were innocent times when we all did that), I walked to Lester's office building and announced that I would live there from now on and never go home to her. He took me home.

He would build a fire and tell me stories while we

watched the flames. Often he would tell me the story of a little flame that went up the chimney in search of adventures: the flame went down onto Tuddington Road, walked to the left, turned right on Weybridge Road, and then left on Hicks Lane . . . and ended up on Middle Neck Road in the town, at the library, at my school. And when the flame got tired of playing in the town, he went down Middle Neck Road until he got to Hicks Lane . . . and down the chimney, safe and sound. And that's how I learned how to find my way home.

Lester usually drove me to school, dropping me off and then continuing to his office. Because we lived at the bottom of a steep hill, he had to put chains on the car tires to get up the hill on snowy days. He taught me to ride a bicycle, though he had never had a bicycle himself as a boy. He learned with me, but never really got the hang of it; mostly he would just run alongside me until I could manage on my own. When he raked autumn leaves, he let me jump into the piles, undoing some of his work that he would cheerfully rake up again. In the summer, we did the same with the grass he raked up after mowing the lawn. To this day, the smell of burning leaves or freshly cut grass always reminds me of Lester. While he was still a smoker (he had smoked all his life, but he gave it up after he had a mild heart attack, in 1960), he used to slip off the cellophane case around the pack of cigarettes and blow smoke into it. When it was quite full, he gave it to me to hold. He blew smoke rings, several in a row so that the new, small ring would sail forth and go through the opening in the older, now expanded ring.

Once when we were swimming at Jones Beach, and I was in the shallow water on my own, a wave knocked me down, and before I could get up and get the water out of my nose, another wave knocked me down, and another. I was sure my life would end right there and then, until Lester charged into the water and pulled me out. For years I had nightmares about the relentless advance of the waves, which in waking life became a metaphor for those moments when things go faster and faster and there is no time to get out. At some of those moments, it was enough for me to ask myself what advice Lester would have given me, or to remember him saying, "Never go on along a path that you've come to doubt, simply because you've already gone so far along it already." When he died, I fell apart, unable to imagine going on without him.

I inherited Lester's respect for religious people, his love of English and American and Russian literature, his weakness for Frazer's *The Golden Bough*. I took after him, went into his business, the world of books, of galley proofs and printers, indeed the world of religion. I also inherited his impatience, his physical clumsiness, his tendency to sulk rather than speak out when he was angry, and his money habits, picking up checks and, going farther than he would ever have gone, handling money in general as Saul Bellow once described Allan Bloom's financial policy: throwing it off the back of a train.

When I grew older, Lester became an important influence on my writing. He was, after all, a successful publisher, a man who knew how to read a manuscript and make it better. He read everything I wrote (I sent him all my notes from India) and invariably loved it. He did not live to see any of my books published, but he had his printer bind in half-calf Moroccan leather my two-volume, nine-hundred-fifty-page 1968 Harvard PhD dissertation. I have an irrational regret that he cannot read this tribute to him.

In the late 1960s, when I was living in Oxford and teaching in London, Lester did a certain amount of publishing with Robert Maxwell, of Pergamon Press, informally known as the "bouncing Czech," a slippery character who eventually vanished off his yacht in mysterious circumstances; the body was later recovered from the water. But the Maxwell connection gave Lester an excuse to visit me in England, and to keep a small but elegant flat above the great restaurant Prunier, in St. James, a flat that I used as a *pied à terre* when I was in London. From time to time, Maxwell sent us very high pheasants from his Scottish estate. But finally, when Maxwell refused to show Lester his financial records, Lester broke off the relationship. Still, he kept the flat above Prunier, and maintained other publishing connections in London, and was often in England.

In those days, the British still used pounds, shillings,

and pence, and Lester never got the knack of the system. Every time he wanted to buy something, he handed them a five (or ten, or hundred) pound note, and put the change in his pocket. By the end of the day, his pockets were bursting with coins, and he waddled back to his hotel like a mule laden with saddlebags. Whenever he came to visit us in Oxford, he brought us a present. On one occasion, as he handed us a small box, he remarked that he had taken his usual early morning walk in St. James that day and come across a nice little shop, where he had bought the gift. I opened it; it was a set of gorgeous gold and enamel demi-tasse spoons from Garrard the Crown Jewelers.

One strange part of my legacy from Lester surfaced years later, in 2010, when I wrote several books about Hinduism that brought me into direct conflict with reactionary Hindu forces in India and the United States. One of the books, the target of a lawsuit that sought to stop its publication and destroy all copies in India, became what Hamlet might have called a pulpable hit. There were many attacks on me by the Hindu right (and defenses from the left).[23] One of the attacking articles focused on me but incidentally swiped at Lester and Rita and cited the Congressional Record. Getting the facts, here and elsewhere, upside down, the writer accused all three of us of being not Communists but, *au contraire*, CIA agents. In with all the rest of the garbage was a widely repeated charge that I was a Christian missionary. When I protested that, whatever you might say of me, you really couldn't say I was a Christian missionary, since I was and always had been Jewish, I was greeted with an appalling barrage of antisemitic attacks, such as this email: "I don't know much about jews. Based on your work, I think jews are evil. So Hitler was probably correct in killing all jews in Germany."[24] I had been better off as a Christian missionary.

But that particular libel inspired one such attacker to link me with Lester: "A fervent believer in converting people to Christianity, Lester Doniger actively helped evangelical churches achieve this goal. Together with his brother Simon Doniger, he published two journals — *Pulpit Digest* and *Pastoral Psychology* — in order to help the Christian churches become more powerful and efficient in their operations."[25] My uncle Simon was also invoked in the attacks on me: "Even the idea of mixing up sex and religion did not originate with her. Her uncle Simon Doniger had published a book titled *Sex and Religion Today.* . . . Wendy Doniger continued where Simon Doniger had left off and her work was aligned with the message of Christian missionaries and SIECUS packaged in academic verbiage and style."

So the overheated imagination of the Hindu right-wing trolls was haunted by a kind of Doniger Dynasty of Porn and Proselytizing, not to mention the insinuation that my scandalous ideas were not even original, but came from my elder male relatives.

Lester remains my ideal, imagined reader to this day; his voice is still strong in my ears. It encourages me to take risks, to have confidence that I will find some readers who will get my jokes, love the stories that I love, and respect my opinions even when they do not share them. I sound out every line I write, imagining the reader reading it, and never imagining as the reader a certain sort of scholar who might be watching with an eagle eye, poised to pounce on any mistake I might make. No, I always imagine the reader as my father, on my side. And I try to be that person to my students, who are otherwise vulnerable to an *imaginaire* of hostile reception that can block their writing, as it keeps some of my most brilliant colleagues from publishing. Lester saved me from that.

My (second) husband once remarked, wryly, "There are easier things in life than to be married to the daughter of Lester Doniger." When I finally divorced and reverted to my maiden name again, one of my best friends, who knew me well from nursery school days right on through Radcliffe and still today, said, "You finally succeeded in marrying your father."

My Relationship with Rita during Her Life

Lewis Carroll was Rita's Bible, and she raised me so that it is my Bible too. When I was still very young, perhaps six or seven, she gave me copies of *Alice in Wonderland* and *Through the Looking-Glass*. The Red Queen, who believed that she was always right about everything and brooked no disagreement, strongly reminded me of Rita. (Once, I accused her of never ever admitting that she was wrong. "Nonsense," she said, "I would certainly change my opinion if someone else showed me a better one. But no one ever has.") And the White Queen, who always suffered catastrophes before they happened ("Ouch! Ouch! I'm going to prick my finger!"), became for me, throughout my life, a way of resisting my own tendency to fall prey to sleepless anxiety about things that might never happen. Another author that Rita taught me to love was Robert Benchley, from whom I learned Benchley's Law: "Anyone can do any amount of work, provided it isn't the work he is supposed to be doing at that moment."[26] This has been the guiding principle of my working/nonworking life: there is always some work that I can do in order not to do some other piece of work.

Rita also fed me books with socialist/Communist messages. From Russian War Relief, I had books about jolly Russian peasant women working in the fields with their jolly children. One of these, *My Mother Is the Most Beautiful Woman in the World* (1945), was about a little Ukrainian girl who gets separated from her fat, round-faced mother, and tells all the people who help find her that her mother is the most beautiful woman in the world. Inside the back cover was a space that invited me to place a picture of my mother, "the most beautiful woman in the world." Rita also gave me books about China and Japan. When I was seven, in 1947, she gave me Pearl Buck's *The Big Wave*, about a child whose family is wiped out by a tsunami. For years I had nightmares about being chased by a great wave that towered above me and was about to fall on me as I ran from it, the wave growing higher and higher in direct geometric proportion to my more slowly increasing distance from its base, so that no matter how fast and far I ran, the wave was going to fall right on me. Sometimes this image got mixed up with my other oceanic nightmare, the dream of the relentless stream of waves that kept knocking me down. Sometimes I could work it in my dream so that Lester came along and pulled me out from under the shadow of the escalating geometric wave.

Rita gave me books about India. When I was about twelve, she gave me E. M. Forster's *A Passage to India*, which seared my soul. It's one of the books that I read in a single twenty-four-hour binge, and that I remember exactly where I was when I read it: in my room in our house, where I stayed up all the hot, humid summer night, with all the windows open, listening to the crickets and the moaning of the foghorns in Long Island Sound, and then to the birdsong in the morning. It made me want to study India, to go to India, to go into those caves that Forster described. Throughout the years, key insights and metaphors from Forster played a pivotal role in my own books, starting with *Other Peoples' Myths: The Cave of Echoes* (1988). Rita also gave me books by Rumer Godden and a copy of Aubrey Menen's newly published, wickedly satirical retelling of the ancient Sanskrit epic, the *Ramayana* (1954). I didn't know then that Menen's book had already been banned in India under Indian Penal Code 295A, and of course I could not know that I myself would run headlong into that same law over half a century later.

When I was little, in the cold mornings I would climb into bed with Rita, who was always warm; she would close my cold hands under her warm armpits as she dozed. And when she had asthma, as she usually did, I would put my ear to her chest and listen to the people talking inside her chest, which is what I made of the wheezing noises. When I was sick in bed myself, and feverish, thrashing my covers into a sweaty tangle, she would come in and pull the covers off and stand at the foot of the bed, and, holding the bottom of each sheet or blanket, throw it high in the air over me so that it billowed like a sail, making a delicious wind on my face, and let it float down on me, smooth and cool, banishing my fever.

Rita sewed most of my clothes on a Singer sewing machine with a treadle that she powered with her foot. She could look carefully at a suit or dress that she saw someone wearing at a public occasion, and go home and cut it out with pieces of brown paper, and then with cloth, and reproduce it. She made my costume when I was five and played Mustardseed in *A Midsummer Night's Dream* at Adelphi College. She made my tutu when I was eight and in ballet school, and again when I was fifteen, and she made my dress for the senior prom out of a soft golden material, shirred over the bodice like a dirndl.

TRYING NOT TO BE LIKE RITA

And yet as a child, I always thought of her as my worst enemy. My agonistic relationship with her began at my birth, when she named me Wendy Turkey Doniger, because I was born on Thanksgiving Day in 1940. (Needless to say, I dropped the middle name as soon as I was old enough to comprehend its existence, but it remains engraved on the little silver cup and matching napkin ring that my uncle Juny gave me on the occasion of my birth, and I sometimes use the "T" when I need a middle initial.)

As I grew up, I wanted to be like Lester and not like Rita. I always wished that my aunt Irma (Simon's wife, Ann's mother, a literary, soft-spoken, tactful woman) was my mother instead of Rita, and Ann said that she sometimes wished that Rita (whom she found eccentric and fascinating) was her mother instead of Irma (whom she found dull).

Instead of admiring Rita for recycling and composting long before anyone else, I was ashamed, because the neighbors complained about the compost and I was disgusted by what I regarded as a lot of smelly garbage. It embarrassed me that she never did what other people did. She was supremely practical, a great devotee of William Morris: "Form follows function," she always used to say, and dressed me in trousers that she made on that Singer sewing machine. I hated them; I wanted to wear store-bought skirts like all the other girls. Rita still boasted of those trousers during our NPR interview in 1990, and I still objected. She said, "I never did what all the other mothers did for their children. When we lived in Great Neck they all got sick in the cold because it was the style for children to wear little short dresses. I thought this was insane. And you couldn't buy the things, so I made trousers and pants for her, and she was never sick. The others all were." (Me: "I was constantly sick.") "No, you never were." (Me: "I was constantly sick. This is one of my mother's mythologies.")

I similarly resisted the liverwurst sandwiches on whole-wheat bread that she packed for my school lunches, sandwiches that both my brother Tony and I threw away. I always threw mine into a particular vacant lot on Hick's Lane, and kept checking in fear that a liverwurst tree would grow there. Lester was complicit in this, secretly giving us lunch money to buy food at school; we bought cream cheese and jelly sandwiches on white bread. I always felt that Lester's complicity in giving us money to circumvent the liverwurst sandwiches at school was closely related to his mother's surreptitious disruption of the *milchig/ fleischig* rules in Raczki. (Liverwurst on whole wheat is now one of my favorite foods.)

I consciously resolved to be *not* like her, not to cook or garden. To this day, I can barely sew on a button when it falls off. Did she offer to teach me and I refused, because I didn't want to be like her, didn't want to be a housewife — having learned *that* lesson from her? Or did she not want me to cook — and, if so, why? Because she wanted to remain supreme in that area? Because she didn't want me to be a housewife, limited as she had been limited? I honestly don't know, but I lean toward the last hypothesis. (Though I did learn from her to cook one great thing, her cheesecake, which I make for students, colleagues, and family for all important and also not-so-important gatherings. But it is *very* easy to make. See Appendix 3.)

Rita gave me good advice that I didn't take. She warned me never to wear scrappy underwear in case I was in an accident and had to ride in an ambulance, and one hot summer day half a century later, I had a heart attack and did have to ride in the ambulance and was very very sorry that I was wearing such ratty underwear.

So much of my personality was formed in direct opposition to her. For instance, Rita would never buy anything that was not on sale — food, clothing, a car, a work of art, anything. And so I never got what I really wanted; if I wanted a red coat, I had to wait for the clearance sale at the end of the season, and then they only had green coats left, so I got a green coat. Ricocheting away from Rita to the point of neuroticism, I am actually incapable of buying anything at bargain prices; if something I want happens to be on sale, I wait for the sale to end and buy it at full price. If food is reduced in price in a supermarket, I assume that it is damaged goods and I buy, instead, another brand that is not on sale. In part, too, I share Lester's assumption that if something is more expensive, it's likely to be better. I *know* this isn't true but I can't help doing it. In large part, I'm just going as far as possible in the opposite direction from Rita.

So, too, I am not only always on time, as Lester was, but I am trapped in an exaggerated overcompensation for Rita's chronic lateness. She imprinted me in my youth, when, living in a suburb with no public transport, I had no choice but to wait for her to drive me everywhere. By the time I got to birthday parties, they had invariably already cut the birthday cake. By the time we got to movie houses or theaters, the show had already begun, and we had to find our seats in the dark, as people grumpily let us by.

Rita picked me up after school every day and drove me to the railroad station so that I could catch the train to New York for my ballet classes with George Balanchine. But by the time she picked me up, not only had all the students left, but even the teachers had gone home, expressing some concern for me as I waited all alone. Often Rita was so late that I missed the train in Great Neck, and she would drive me at breakneck speed to pick up the subway in Flushing. I would arrive at ballet class after they had finished the work at the bar, and I had to warm up by myself. Nowadays, therefore, I always get to the airport, and the theater, and the restaurant long before any reasonable person would be there. (The White Queen always pounces on me at these times: "What if there's an accident and/or a traffic jam on the expressway? What if you can't find a place to park?") I always used to bring a book to read as I waited; nowadays, there's Kindle on my cell phone.

Rita was a perverse influence on me in other ways, as well. During one period of my life, I translated Rita's food-keeping habits into my sex life. She would keep food until it became garbage, and then it was okay to throw it out because you weren't throwing out food, just garbage. Adapting that model, I used to keep a boyfriend around for a while when I had tired of him but it seemed cruel to get rid of him when he was still keen on me. To make the break, I waited until it was clear that the relationship had become garbage, so that I couldn't blame myself for throwing him out.

That's about the only aspect of my sex life that Rita ever contributed to. She didn't want me to marry, but if I did, she wanted me to marry an orphan (presumably with no in-laws for her to compete with). Or, better, she wanted me to have a baby out of wedlock and give it to her to raise. When I did marry, at the age of twenty, of course the only way I could rebel against such a rebellious mother was to do something completely conventional: so I married a nice Jewish boy — who was going to be a *doctor* — in a very fancy wedding at the Plaza Hotel, with a *huppe* and a rabbi, and my picture in the *New York Times*, and the whole nine yards. Before, during, and after this marriage, Rita referred to my husband only as Mr. Wrong, and she was, as usual, right. She offered to give me several thousand dollars if I'd just elope, but I refused. Then she refused to go to the wedding; she had, she said, tickets for *Lohengrin* that day. When Lester prevailed upon her to attend, she did. When, after just a year, I divorced Mr. Wrong,* she immediately said, "For this I gave up my tickets to *Lohengrin*?" (Actually, in going through Rita's notes now, I found that she had saved a card I had sent her, saying, "Thank you for coming to my wedding instead of going to *Fliegender Holländer*." So that was the opera, not *Lohengrin*. But the story has been told in our family for years with *Lohengrin* as the opera, so I won't change it now.)

Time passed. I married the man I should have married in the first place, someone Rita liked very much, my high school sweetheart, an Irish American named O'Flaherty. We moved to Oxford in 1965. When Lester died, in 1971, Rita discovered, like many widows, that people she had regarded as *their* friends turned out to have been *his* friends and drifted away from her. As she remarked in a note, "With age we widen the circle of our acquaintances and narrow the

---

*Lester went with me to Mexico, to Juarez, as one had to do to get a New York divorce without consent, in 1960, and on return he had a mild heart attack.

circle of friends." Lester was the one who had made most of the friends that they shared; Rita had chosen to spend much of her time alone. And now she was really alone. She wrote about this in her notes on Christmas Day, 1975: "I feel like a ghost at the social gatherings. I speak, I interpolate, but it is unheard and unnoticed. The conversations and repartee continue smoothly as though uninterrupted. There is no response. The aphorisms, the witticisms are ignored, unheard or disregarded, and eventually the feeling of being invisible prevails and I am quenched."

Rita came to Oxford to be with me when our son Mike was born, a few months after Lester's death. She was suddenly without the main job she had been doing for the past three decades — the job of Lester Doniger's wife — so she seized upon a possible new career: raising my child. Contemplating my clumsy attempts to be a good wife and mother, she said, "It astonishes me to see that you have become Dora" (the helpless child-wife in *David Copperfield*). She devoted herself to proving to me that I could not raise a child by myself, something I was inclined to believe even without her telling me. How could I possibly do this enormous new task without Lester's help? I distinctly remember thinking, brutally, that the wrong parent had died. This was the low point of my relationship with Rita. In the end, we got a nanny and Rita returned to Great Neck.

But by that time, a combination of postpartum depression (I had been hospitalized for several months with preeclampsia and then had an emergency Caesarian after thirty-six hours of labor), grieving for Lester, and the belief (nourished by Rita) that anyone else would do a better job of raising my child, made me suicidal. (The final straw was my failure, during this same period, to find a publisher for my first book; apparently I couldn't even do *that* well.[27]) My doctor put me into Warneford Hospital (first named the Oxford Lunatic Asylum in 1826, later Warneford Lunatic Asylum). They actually still did basket weaving there, and when I protested that it was a waste of my time, they let me bring in my typewriter (a red IBM Correcting Selectric), and there, during the basket-weaving period, I wrote much of my book about evil in Indian mythology,[28] simultaneously working through my own first personal experience of evil. Eventually I was discharged by a wise psychiatrist, a Holocaust survivor, who once told me, "If you commit suicide now, you'll be sorry later," and assured me, as I left and asked her if she thought I'd end up back there again, "I think you will never again experience simultaneously the death of your father and the birth of your first child." And she was right.

In 1975 we moved from Oxford to Berkeley, and both my career and my marriage started to fall apart. I flew to Great Neck to ask Rita's advice, and she was supportive and wise; she urged me not to remain in what had become a destructive relationship. (Was she thinking of her own marriage? I never knew.) I returned to Berkeley, left the marriage, and took Mike (and the dachshund and the Siamese lynx-point cat) with me to Chicago in 1978, where I had a full professorship in the Divinity School of the University of Chicago. Now I was a single mother, and Rita came to stay with Mike while I went to a conference in New Orleans. I returned to find Mike in fine shape — he always did get along well with Rita — but the house entirely transformed. Rita had taken advantage of my absence to organize all the kitchen cabinets and all the closets and drawers in the house, putting all my possessions, which I had been keeping in the *wrong* place, in the *right* place. For months after that, I was unable to find anything I wanted, and there is one jacket that I have never ever been able to find to this day.

RITA'S ATTITUDE TOWARD
MY WORK ON RELIGION

While she was in Chicago, Rita came to my inaugural lecture, sat in the front row, and fell fast asleep. My colleagues in the Divinity School found her absolutely charming, which was a great relief to me; I had been rather nervous about introducing her to them, given her attitude toward religion. Lester had worked closely with the pastors of the local Episcopal and Catholic churches in our largely Jewish town. I met these men at his office from time to time, and he frequently lunched with them in Great Neck or New York. But, recalling the space-helmet episode and

Rita's anticlericalism, he knew better than to bring them home. I now shared his misgivings.

But in fact, Rita had played a strange, by no means entirely negative role in the development of my own relationship to religion. I had become, by the age of eight or nine, intensely interested in religious questions. I wondered how, if there was a God, the world could be in the mess it was in, and then I began to wonder if there was a God at all, and then why anyone believed that there was a God. I asked to go to Hebrew school; I wanted to read the Bible in Hebrew. Rita couldn't have been more shocked if I had announced that I wanted to start mainlining heroin. But they sent me to Temple Beth-el. There, alas, I quickly discovered that they seemed to do nothing but raise money to plant trees in Israel. And I had hoped to see the face of God (or at least to learn to read Hebrew). So I left, to the patent relief of Rita. I honestly cannot remember if Lester was glad or sad about it.

The great current of my fascination with religion was thus diverted, quite early, from the Judaism that was my birthright to other religions in which I was always just poaching. I hung out with Christians; I eventually married a Christian. But I always knew I was Jewish. When, in 1964, I was in a horrendous automobile accident, which smashed in a piece of my skull and broke several arms and legs, I nevertheless remained conscious and answered the questions they asked me as I was admitted to the emergency room. When they asked, "Religion?" I said, "Jewish." I was in the hospital for three months, and during that time I was plagued by a rabbi who wanted to talk to me about my faith, and urged me to attend services, and wore me out. So when I returned to the hospital for some remedial surgery a while later, upon check-in I put down, for religion, "Hindu," thinking, well, that will keep the rabbi away. It did, but now I was plagued by a nun who was even more tenacious than the rabbi. On one occasion, she asked me, "When did you first embrace the Hindu faith, Mrs. O'Flaherty?" So I told her I was Jewish, and she left me alone. Years later, when the Hindu fundamentalists accused me of being a Christian missionary and I assured them that I was, actually, Jewish, I thought of Rita's statement: Hitler made me a Jew. That nun and the Hindu fanatics made me a Jew in a way that the rabbi never could.

One might have expected Rita to object to my ending up in a divinity school. But she didn't. When, during our NPR interview she was asked how, given her views of religion, she felt about the fact that I made my living writing about religious texts, she replied, "Wendy? You're not religious, are you? I didn't know she was! [laughs heartily] The first I — do you believe in god? Or did you believe in god? As a child?" When asked about the myths that I write about, she replied, "If they'll believe that, they'll believe *any-thing*!" When I persisted and asked, "What do you think of the fact that I have spent the last twenty-five years writing books about myths?" she replied, "Well, you just liked it. And also you were very bright, very brilliant. But I think it's all made up in your mind. It's a creation. Like a detective story. [Me: "Do you think I wasted my life?"] Oh no! No, you created something. But it has nothing to do with truth, with reality. No, no. Not at all. But it's fun, and you enjoyed it. And people believe you!" [She laughs heartily.]

AMBIVALENCE AND RECONCILIATION

Rita used two different accounting systems in valuing me: to other people, she credited my success simultaneously to both accounts, increasing hers as well as mine, so that Rita = Rita's Achievement + Wendy's Achievement. But when we were alone together, suddenly it was a world of limited good, in which Achievement was a single sum divided into Rita's + Wendy's, my weaknesses making her stronger. Therefore she exaggerated my accomplishments when relating them to other people, my grades in school and the praise that Balanchine is alleged to have given me when I was a dancer. And then she turned around and, to my face, pointed out how badly I drew or played the piano. When I was young, I complained that she never praised me for anything I did, that she was always critical of me. She replied that she didn't want me to become complacent, to have a swelled head; she wanted me always to strive to do better; and I do. She always kept all my books on the little table beside her bed (paradigm A), but she never read any of them (paradigm B). Or, rather, she told me that she never read any of them, that she thought they would be too difficult for her.

By the time I went to Radcliffe, her envy of my academic achievements got its nose in front in the race with her pride in those same achievements, and we became not companions in crime, but competitors. For a part of her resented me for doing precisely what she had wanted me to do, for succeeding as a scholar. She had put all her energies into forming me instead of using them in the career she so desperately wanted — though it was never clear to me precisely what that career would have been. Her regret built on a deeper, earlier set of resentments: against her father for keeping her home to raise her siblings so that she could not go to college, against her sisters for going to college, against Lester for going to college. (When she was dying, and floating in and out of reality, she said she felt sorry for Lester because he had never finished high school.)

As I grew older, and Rita, oddly enough, grew older too, we became better friends. She came to visit me when I was in India in 1963; Lester had intended to come too, but suddenly got embroiled in a business crisis that he could not walk away from, so she came alone, the first time she had traveled alone in decades. She arrived in Madras after a very long flight (no jets yet in those days) and climbed down the steps from the plane holding in one hand her purse and in the other a New York kosher salami, wrapped up in crinkly aluminum foil salvaged from something or other. It was what she felt I most needed in India.

She was a good sport throughout the trip, and let me make all the plans (Figure 32). She traveled with me to see the temples at Bhubaneshwar and Puri. We stayed at a seaside hotel with cockroaches the size of hamsters; she was fascinated and delighted by them, and indeed never complained about anything on the whole trip. We went up into the hills near Madras to a village where strolling actors were performing scenes from the *Mahabharata*. They served us some very suspicious-looking food, which I, who had been suffering on and off from dysentery (both amoebic and bacillary) all year, politely declined. Rita, who never in her life passed up a free meal, reached for it. I shook my head decisively at her, looking daggers at the food. She smiled at me and ate it all and perversely did not get sick. She went on from India to see Angkor Wat at last (in 1964, with the Vietnam War already lapping at the borders of Cambodia—nothing could stop her). And she wrote to me from Cambodia: "I know it gave you pleasure to manage and protect me, darling, and I let you mother me. But I am really quite able to manage alone, tho I concede at once traveling alone is more difficult unless empty handed, and Ah for Nataraja's arms! What a travel companion he would make!"

Much later, she recalled that visit to India and Angkor as the high point of her entire life.

My Relationship with Rita after She Died

After Lester's death and Mike's birth, Rita visited us in Oxford several times; she was there when I received my D Phil, in 1973 (Figure 33). After we returned to America, in 1975, I visited her often in Great Neck. She would meet me at LaGuardia, as she had always done when I flew home from Radcliffe (and Harvard and Oxford and Moscow and Berkeley), and the cool, stony, quiet house would greet me as it had for over a quarter of a century. Once home, she would often ignore me and return to the routine that she followed when she was alone, mostly watching television (*Columbo* and *Kojak* and *The Rockford Files*). So I watched television with her, as I had done for so many years. Eventually, there was someone there to help look after her.

Sometimes I took her shopping, or to a medical appointment. By this time she was rather unsteady on her feet, and I kept hold of her as we walked. On one of those occasions, when the appointment was over, I asked her if she was able to lean against the wall of the medical building while I went into the parking lot and brought the car around; she assured me that she could do that. I walked away, and immediately she fell forward onto her face, and a pool of blood started to form around her head. I rushed to her, fearing that she was dead, and thinking, "What am I going to tell Tony?" I was relieved to find that she was okay; it was a minor nosebleed that quickly abated. But

I knew I should not have let her talk me into leaving her alone even for a moment. I had failed to care for her, another low point in my checkered career as Rita's daughter.

During the last five years of her life, Rita took to her bed. In a very real sense, that's when she died to the world. I began to become fully reconciled to her, and she to me, only after she had signed off in that way. When she was finally near death, she told me that she loved me. She had never said that before, though she had written it in some of her letters to me. That was when I realized that she knew she was dying.

After she died, I began to appreciate what she had done for me and how much I owed to her. Indeed, already in my teens, my embarrassment at her unconventional behavior had begun to be tempered by an admiration for her, even a pride in the ways that she was not like everyone else's mothers. Even my decision to study Sanskrit at the age of seventeen was largely her doing, not only because she had taught me to love India, but also because she had taught me to plough my own furrow; *no one* in the freshman year at Radcliffe or Harvard was majoring in Sanskrit. But only after her death did I begin to realize that I had inherited my perversity, perversely, from Rita, so that whenever I disobeyed her or rebelled against her, I was doing precisely what she would have done in my place, and therefore I was *not* rebelling against her. And I began to appreciate that I had also inherited from her my pride in standing against the mob. When I became embroiled in the struggle against the right-wing Hindus, fighting for my book but also fighting for my publisher, my reflexive thought was that my father the publisher was standing me in good stead. No, said my son Mike, grandma is standing by you.

Getting to Be More Like Rita

Suddenly I found that I was living Rita's life after all. Like a character in the recognition narratives I wrote about in *The Woman Who Pretended to Be Who She Was*, like Viola, or Oedipus, I realized who I was: not my father, but my mother. I am like her more and more as I grow older and I change into her and also realize ways, both trivial and profound, in which I was always like her and just didn't see it — or didn't let myself see it. On the banal level, Rita had nothing but scorn for people who followed the latest fashion, who wore what everyone else was wearing. She always insisted on dressing herself and me (when I was small) in clothes that were loose, comfortable, free flowing, often unflattering, and never ever fashionable. Now I, too, look with silent disapproval at the painfully tight jeans and the impossibly high stacked heels, and I dress mostly in black stretch pants and black jersey tops from L.L. Bean (the closest thing there is to leotard and tights). (Just as Catherine Deneuve was always said to be "Dressed by Chanel" and Audrey Hepburn "Dressed by Givenchy," so I am "Dressed by L.L. Bean.") My particular fashion signature is black with white dog hair.

Now that I am just a few years short of the age at which she died, I realize that I have Rita's no-holds-barred sense of humor and her disregard for social customs and for minor legal regulations that I don't believe in. I channel her every time I turn on the radio before getting out of bed, and I apologize to her ghost every time I throw out a bit of food. She took over when I decided to let the land around my house in Truro grow wild, like the "jungle" that she let grow up in front of our house in Great Neck. I recognize as hers my obsessive need to put everything in the kitchen in the *right place*. Rita takes over me when I find myself taking compulsive pleasure in fitting one packing box into another and then into another, even just to take them to the dump. I even got fat, like her.

But there has also been a strange skewing of the generational preferences. The avant-garde that she so loved, against the prevailing classical fashion, in her youth included Richard Strauss and Dixieland jazz. I inherited her specific tastes, for Strauss and Dixieland and much else, but I hung onto them and stayed with them. I didn't move forward from Strauss to Stockhausen and from Dixieland to Charlie Parker, as Rita did. Thoroughly imbued with her once "modern" tastes, but without a taste for the modern, I became old-fashioned.

Of course, it's more complicated than that. Like most children, I had four options: to be like her, to be like him, to be *not* like her, to be *not* like him. In some ways I am a dichotomous monster compounded of both of them, combining Rita's I-don't-care-what-anyone-else-thinks attitude with Lester's need to have everyone love him, a difficult combination to live with. (In this I resemble my favorite mythological beast, Woody Allen's Great Roe, who has the head of a lion and the body of a lion, but not the same lion.[29]) I became rebellious in spirit (like her), but conservative in my tastes (like him), an in-your-face traditionalist, in my life as well as my academic work.

The main problem of my relationship with Rita was that I met her when I was too young to appreciate her. Since she always had to be right, everyone else wrong, I had to fight her for my own opinions every day of my childhood, without pausing to consider that she might, sometimes, be right. Moreover, I met her in an epoch before there were terms in which to appreciate her. A few decades later, I would have perceived her eccentricities so differently; she would have been a feminist hero. When I look back on Rita now from the vantage point of third-wave feminism, I see that she was a woman of our time, not of hers; but neither she nor I could have known that then. She embarrassed me as a child precisely because she refused to be a woman of that earlier, benighted time. And now that she is gone, and there is no need to fight, I have the advantage of having known her without the disadvantage of having to protect myself from her.

When I gave the series of lectures at Brandeis University that formed the basis of this present book, the person who (without consulting me) made the poster advertising the lecture misread my list of illustrations and put on the poster not a photograph of me, but a photograph of Rita. There it was in print: I had become my mother. More precisely, I had become not my mother but what she wanted me to become, and what she herself would have wanted to become had she had the chances that she had given to me.

The full force of the family personality skipped my generation, as it often does, and landed on my son Mike, who, though named after Lester (Michael Lester O'Flaherty), takes after Rita in some ways even more than I do. Mike inherited her habit of staying up half the night and sleeping until noon; ever since his teens, I have often met him going up to bed at 5:00 a.m. when I was going down to start the day, just as I used to meet her. Mike was at NYU (Lester's alma mater) during Rita's final years, and often visited her in Great Neck; they became good friends. And he inherited her politics: he wrote his BA dissertation at NYU on the Jews in the Abraham Lincoln Brigade of the Spanish Civil War, Rita's first great cause. The Abraham Lincoln Brigade Archives awarded him a prize for it, but they couldn't locate him to give it to him. A few years went by, and a member of ALBA was at a dinner with Rita's sister Elsie (who had married a man that Rita had met at a Communist Party meeting and brought home). Someone mentioned that they had failed to find this Mike O'Flaherty to give him his prize. Elsie spoke up: "That's my nephew!" and through her, they eventually found him. Mike also inherited Rita's talent for doggerel (see Postlude).

There is a photograph that Rita kept beside her bed in her final decade (Figure 34). It is a picture of me holding Mike when he was newborn, when Rita and I clashed so destructively. My face gazing into his eyes is smiling with a combination of irony, motherly love, puzzlement, worry, and pride. Why is this the picture of me that she loved best? Did the image become a mirror for her? Can it become a two-way mirror for me now? When I look at that photograph now, I see a picture simultaneously of me and of Rita — because it was the way she saw me then, as herself: a mother. And so I see her (in me) when I look at it. Once, in absentmindedness, I called Michael "Mommy," because he was the one who called me "Mommy." (I also sometimes call him by the name of my dog Kim, or my younger brother Tony, and I sometimes call them all "Mike," equating all the young creatures that I love.) That kind of reciprocity is reflected in a wonderful Sanskrit word, *tata*, which a little boy uses to address an old man ("Grandpa") or an old man to address a little boy ("Sonny"); it means the relationship between the very young and old, in either direction. (The Yiddish *tatele* is similarly symmetrical.) That photograph has the same sort of reciprocity for me.

On Rita's birthday, June 9, in 2001, ten years after her death, I had a dream that I wrote down as soon as I woke up. Its general form was that of the recurrent nightmare that has plagued me all my life: I'm lost in a foreign country, and late for a train or plane, and I can't remember the address of the place where I need to be. But this time it was different; this time I accused Rita of doing precisely what, in waking life, I had hated her for doing:

> I am supposed to make a 10:00 a.m. plane at Logan Airport, and Rita, middle-aged, is supposed to drive me. We are late; she won't leave; I am anxious. I ask her why she has delayed; she says she was admiring the darling little baby in the room. I shout at her in anger: "It's because women always do that, are by nature inclined to do that, that men, instead of women, have always ruled the world." We start driving, but get lost in the streets around the airport. Finally she turns down a street where all the cars are coming toward us, and cars are parked on both sides of the street pointing toward us. I shout at her, she's going the wrong way, and she parks, nose to nose with one of the parked cars. I see that it is after 10:00, that we have missed the plane. Then I see

a sign, an arrow, pointing in the direction that Rita has driven; all the other cars were going the wrong way.

Der Rosenkavalier

In the autumn of 1982, near the end of the time in which Rita was still able to get to New York for the opera, I went with her to see *Der Rosenkavalier* at the Met, with Kiri Te Kanawa as the Marschallin, Tatiana Troyanos as Oktavian, Judith Blegen as Sophie. When the Marschallin sang of getting up in the middle of the night and stopping the clocks, I thought of Rita's nocturnal life. At last came the finale, the great trio, and the three women stopped acting toward one another and stepped forward, squaring themselves to the audience, everyone full of anticipation of the music to come, the most beautiful passage in all opera. They began to sing. The Marschallin renounced her own hope for the love of Oktavian and was content to let the young Sophie have him instead.

As we drove home to Great Neck, I thought to myself that what was at stake for me and Rita was not, as it was for the Marschallin and Sophie, the love of a man, not even really the love of Lester, though it had seemed like that sometimes. What was at stake was a woman's right to become who she was, to have a career instead of (in her day, or in addition to, in mine) raising children. I realized then that Rita had finally given up her hopes for herself, for the life she would have wanted to have, and so had also given up her resentment of me for having had what she had hoped for. At the end of *Rosenkavalier*, for the Marschallin it's all over, but for Sophie, it's all just about to happen. And for me, too, still in my early forties, much of it was yet to happen.

Rita's Comic and Tragic Legacy

The Family Punch Lines

Every family has its own mythology; ours was more comic than tragic. Things that Rita said, and stories that she told, filtered into a corpus that we all knew and could call up on any occasion, often to get us through sticky situations or even to pull us through a tragic moment and turn it into a joke — Viennese *Galgenhumor* again. Usually just the punch line was enough to do the trick. Here are nine of them.

1 Two Jewish ladies in ancient Rome were watching the Christians being thrown to the lions. One of the two ladies began to weep, and the other said, "Why are you crying? For once, it's not the Jews that are getting it. It's the Christians, who have never been friends to us. Why are you crying?" And the weeping lady replied, "One lion isn't eating."

The punch line was a relatively tactful way for Rita to tell one of us to finish what was on our plate.

2 An ad appeared in the *New York Times*: "Wanted for African safari: someone fluent in at least two African

languages, with experience in jungle terrain, knowledge of African geography, and a crack shot." A call came in: "Mister, this is Chaim Schwartz. I'm calling about your ad for the African safari." "Oh good, Mr. Schwartz. How many African languages do you know?" "African? Oh no. Just Yiddish, a little English." "Then is it your experience in Africa that brings you to us?" "Africa, no, no, born in Flatbush, never went anywhere farther than Rockaway Beach." "Your marksmanship?" "You mean guns? Oh no, very dangerous, never touched one." "Then why are you calling us?" "Mister, I only wanted to say: On me you shouldn't count."

The punch line was useful when anyone proposed something like a midnight swim in icy waters, or a long hike over difficult terrain.

3 Moscowitz and Lubowitz had been in business for many years, with the same secretary. Finally she retired, and they hired a new woman, very young and very pretty. Moscowitz took her out one night and reported to Lubowitz the next morning: "Well, we had dinner, a few drinks, then back to her place, a few more drinks, and one thing led to another, and there we were in bed. And the sex was incredible; I never imagined it could be like that; so much better than my wife." So Lubowitz thought he would try his luck, and took the woman out. The next morning they met, and Moscowitz said,

"Nu?" and Lubowitz replied, "Better than your wife I wouldn't say."

This punch line was invoked as a riposte whenever anyone used what Rita regarded as an undeserved superlative —"That was the best strudel I've ever tasted," or "That was the best performance of *Tosca* I ever heard."

4 It was Stalin's birthday, and as the telegrams of congratulations came in, they were read aloud at a meeting of the Comintern. Finally, surprisingly, came one from Trotsky: "Dear Comrade Stalin. I was wrong. You were right. I should apologize." Everyone cheered, until a little Jewish tailor in the front stood up and said, "Comrade Stalin, I fear you didn't read it right. It should go: '*I* was wrong? *You* were right? *I* should apologize?

The last line was particularly useful for those rare moments when someone actually had to admit to being wrong, something neither Rita nor I ever did very well. The joke helped a lot. I still use it with my son.

5 A man's alarm failed to go off on the morning when he had to get to New York from Scarsdale for a very important job interview. He jumped out of bed, already late, and rushed to get ready: he cut himself shaving, bleeding on his only clean shirt; his wife had forgotten to send his shirts to the laundry. His car wouldn't start,

and by the time he called a cab, which came late, and got to the commuter station, the one train that would get him to the interview on time was just pulling out of the station. As he raced to catch it, a little old lady was bending over tying her shoelaces right in front of the gate to the train; he had to slow down to get around her, and *just* missed the train. As he turned to go back home, he saw her, still bent over, and went up to her and kicked her, sending her sprawling onto the ground. "Why did you do that?" she asked, in bewilderment and pain. "You and your damn shoelaces," he replied.

This punch line was always useful to defuse the situation when someone, clearly angry about something else, attacked you unjustly.

6 It seems that Cecil B. DeMille was planning the war epic to end all war epics, and gathered together thousands of people that his team had recruited from hospices and hospitals, people who were soon to die and who had agreed, for a generous sum to be paid to their families or favorite charities, to die, for real, in the course of a spectacular battle scene. The day of the shot, everyone was ready, and DeMille stationed three cameras: one handheld camera for close-ups, one camera for group scenes, and one high on a hill where the cameraman could get a panoramic shot of the whole battle. Lights, camera, action, and the

battle began; after twenty minutes, everyone was dead. DeMille called to the guy with the handheld camera, "Hey, John, what did you get?" "Mr. DeMille, I'm so sorry. This wasn't an ordinary shot; these were real people, not actors. One of them knocked into me and knocked down the camera, and dust got into it and it jammed and I didn't get anything." "Well," said DeMille, "that's a shame, but we still have the other two. Roger [to the man taking the group scenes], how about you?" "Sorry, Mr. DeMille. This was real stuff, not ketchup, real blood; right away some guy bled all over my camera, and by the time I cleaned the lens, it was all over." "Well," said DeMille, "at least we still have the most important view of all. Hey, Joe!" to the guy on the hill. "Ready when you are, Mr. DeMille," came the reply. (There was also a variant punch line: "Ready when you are, C. B.")

This old chestnut was nevertheless frequently very useful; we used it all the time, as a way of reminding Rita, who was always late, that the rest of us were ready, without infuriating her by actually nagging her.

7 "Aside from that, Mrs. Lincoln, how did you enjoy the show?"

This one-liner is useful when someone reports a disastrous experience.

8   This is one of many variants of a Jewish story in which
a rabbi and a priest lock horns in debate, usually on
a train in East Europe, often traveling from Minsk to
Pinsk, and the rabbi makes a fool of the priest. On
this occasion, they meet in the dining car, and the
priest says to the rabbi, "Rabbi, I've always wanted to
know the secret, why your people are so smart." "Oh,
Father," says the rabbi, "it's because we eat fish, and
particular parts of the fish. Let me show you." So they
order a large carp, and the rabbi divides it so that the
priest gets the head and the rabbi gets the rest. The
rabbi assures the priest that the brains, in the head, are
what make the Jews smart. After lunch, the priest says,
"Rabbi, I'm a bit puzzled. All I got was the head, with
hardly anything to eat on it, and you had all the rest of
the fish. But we split the check fifty-fifty. Do you think
that was fair?" To which the rabbi replies, "Ah! The fish
is beginning to work."

"The fish is beginning to work" was often said when
someone finally understood, after a while, something that
the speaker regarded as self-evident.

9   A pious old Jew was dying, surrounded by his loving
family. Near the end, he asked his wife to send for
the priest. Surely, she said, he meant the rabbi; no, he
insisted, the priest, the priest. The priest came and at
the old Jew's request converted him and administered

the final rites. After the priest left, there was weeping and wailing throughout the house, and his wife begged the dying man to tell her why he had done this. With his final breath, he said, "Better one of them should die than one of us."

The last line was often used to express ungenerous satisfaction, Schadenfreude, when something bad happened to an enemy.

Doggerel

In addition to all the stories about Rita, and the oral traditions that she inspired and nourished, on special occasions she produced wonderful doggerel. One such poem was written at the birth of a boy, named James, to her good friends the Coopers, on August 26, 1952:

All hail to James, the best of names,
a monicker so super.
I doff the quill with best of will
to write it before Cooper.
He may have been no kith or kin
to any on Olympus.
But gods have smiled on this new child
and Calliope simpers.
He will compose or quel que chose,
a poet, or a surgeon.
His name in lites will greet our sites;

he'll dine on egg of sturgeon.
He'll not be bored by harpsichord,
no flute or horn will he stop,
but will applaud the music scored
for classical or bebop.
At abstract art he will not fart;
he'll understand the masters.
His poetry, obscure or free,
will pique the poetasters.
Not anymore will Fenimore
top Gallup poll or Hooper.
A newer claim to name of fame
will leave the world in stupor.
P. S. If dancer or singer,
he'll be a humdinger.
I cross me a finger
he'll be a left-winger.

The Coopers remained my parents' best friends through the years. Rita wrote a poem for them on the occasion of some New Year's Eve when she and Lester visited the Coopers in their Scarsdale home at 50 Penn Road:

Dull and dreary is my life
sans the Coopers man and wife.
At home alone could I await
the old year's expiration date?

Not storm not sleet nor gloom nor hail
could separate us from Scarsdale.
Let minstrels shout their carols when
we disembark at 50 Penn
to warm ourselves at blazing hickory,
engage in battle with Terpsichore.
Load the tables, clear the floors,
batten down the bedroom doors,
free the well-kept inhibition
irregardless of attrition.

She wrote a poem on the occasion of her hysterectomy
(see page 65):

The loss of the uterus
Is not so very new to us.
But ominous are the warnings of the ladies who have
experienced this mutilation
Not unlike the male castration,
Of all the dreadful things it will do to us.

The removal of the vagina
Involves a point much finer
And must be viewed askance
By those in pants.

That of the rectum, its severance,
May be endured with perseverance.

> Not since Lister was a pup
> Has the ectomy of hyster been anyone's cup
> Of tea, because the abbreviation of one's fecundity
> Is not considered a source of jocundity.

She also wrote shorter comic poems. This one, from November 1952, is titled "Freud for the Housewife":

> If they ask you for string and you've got it,
> That proves that you're anal erotic.
> If you gain umpteen pounds, then the moral
> Is now you're not anal, you're oral.

Another, undated, has no title (other than the shadow of Lewis Carroll's "You Are Old, Father William"):

> You are old, Father Wolcott, the young man said
> and have grown most uncommonly glib.
> Yet you sharpen your wit on a plagiarized hit.
> Pray, what made you ad lib such a fib?

She wrote a longer poem, somewhat reminiscent of Noel Coward's "Don't Let's Be Beastly to the Germans" (which the BBC banned), after the punitive Nazi annihilation of the Czech village of Lidice in June 1942; it was entitled "Lidice Schmidice":

> Pity the poor German.
> To the Russian he is merman.
> He is spied upon and abused

in a manner to which he is not used.
It will be a calamity
for the rest of humanity
if the Germans in the East
are made to suffer in the least.

They must take political courses
which should fill them with remorses
    for the little errors they in past have made.
And there'll be no more occurrence
of the deeds they show preference
    for, because the Eastern Germans are afraid.
From way back, through the ages,
all the best Teutonic rages
    have spread the word that Germans are the top.
But today the wicked Russians
have impoverished the Prussians
    and the Nazi propaganda has to stop.
In the Western German zone
there prevails a different tone
    and you don't hear Western Germans go
    complaining.
Though he may be unemployed
the good burgher's overjoyed
    For he's undergoing democratic training.

He may vote for whom he will,
and so he picks the Nazi still.

I must confess that the compulsion to commit doggerel seems to have been passed down through me (for I have published limericks[30]) to my son Mike, who, on July 24, 1974, at the tender age of two and a half, produced (orally, for he could not yet write, and was apparently still working hard on his toilet training) two quasi limericks, or perhaps even satires on the limerick form:

There was an old man on the border
who crapped in his cup in the water.
When his friends asked him why,
he said it is my
cup.

There was an old man with some 'bena*
who crapped with the utmost demeanor.
He said to the mice,
"Is it proper or nice
to crap on a cat in the water?"

Rita loved them and recorded them in her notes.

The Silent Archive

There are also other records of Rita's literary output. I lived abroad for over a decade, in an age when long-distance phone calls were largely reserved for emergencies, in our family at least, and she wrote almost a hundred let-

---

*'*Bena* was Mike's way of referring to Ribena, his favorite blackcurrant drink.

ters to me, some of them very long. I carefully saved them in a large box. And there was, in addition, another documentation of her creative mental life, though we didn't know about it during her lifetime.

In all those years when she stayed up all night, she wrote. After she died, we found, stashed in a bureau drawer, a box containing hundreds and hundreds of small pieces of paper, most of them those narrow strips that supermarkets print out with the itemized list of your groceries. There were also some larger sheets, and a few small notebooks (Figure 35). I "lost" them soon after we found them. Freud would certainly have a lot to say about that. But I found them again, a quarter of a century later, just as I began to write this memoir ...

She had covered these pieces of paper with sketches, witty sayings that she had heard or read or made up herself, critical reviews of plays and books and concerts, diatribes against conventional society, notes on the history of Chinese art and pre-Columbian art, ideas for short stories, meditations on art, history, music, freedom, politics, love, sex, the raising of children, and much, much more. Her observations about people are often quite sharp, the makings of a novel she never got to write. I have drawn on these writings, and on her letters to me, throughout this present memoir, and a sampling of them is reproduced in Appendix 2.

She never showed any of this to any of us, even when

we were grown up; she may have written the notes to herself, or to god knows who. This archive remained as private, as solipsistic, as her nocturnal séances. Perhaps her inward, solitary habits were by then too ingrained for her to share her writings. The very fact of the existence of these notes speaks to us of Rita's loneliness, her feeling that she had no one to talk to. She says as much, in one note (dated January 17, 1966), a long letter to Edward Albee, about his play "Tiny Alice." Rita says, "You not only spoke thoughts I have often harbored but expressed them even as I would. It was like hearing myself talk, a practice I am frequently reduced to due to a paucity of empathetic listeners." She used to wander around the house at night muttering, "Je ne suis pas contente," like Rousseau's Eloise. In one of her notes, her feeling of extreme alienation took the form of a *Looking-Glass* fantasy: "I cherish the illusion I am in a make-believe world, a fantasy, looking thru windows at the *real* world. The dramas, playlets, events I witness are all *real*, and *I* am the vision, the fiction — who can say? — my nose pressed to the glass like Lucius Beebe's urchin. I observe the goings on of the world of real people from my seat outside."

In another note, she writes that Mozart and Hemingway kept the whole of their great work in their heads until they felt it was perfect and ready to come out, and then they wrote it all down. Did Rita write these notes hoping that some day, like Mozart and Hemingway, she too would find a way to write it all down, that some day it would become complete in her head and then come out? Or that someday someone would find these scraps? Or did she mean them to remain forever private, in which case I am violating her wishes in publishing some of them now?

Some of the scribblings are banal, like a high school student's class notes, or undigested information about subjects that interested her, such as pre-Columbian art history. And yet every once in a while, there is something wonderful, and the sad thing is that she didn't know the difference between them. Lorraine Daston, a friend of mine and a historian who works in archives, lit up like a Christmas tree when she saw Rita's archive. She realized its meaning, and in a 2017 email commented that these pieces of paper are Exhibit A for "the obvious waste of a good mind and the loneliness of having no one to talk to about her interests in art, philosophy, or literature. On the other hand, the writing itself is testimony to the fact that she didn't just retreat into silent melancholy; she wrote for herself, at least." What troubles me most about the archive is that Rita didn't think that her thoughts were valuable enough to write on brand-new paper. She wrote it all on scraps that she was recycling, saving; she wrote it on what other people regarded as garbage. Of course, this was in keeping with her general dedication to economizing and recycling, but there is more to it, too. There is a telling meditation about all of this in one of the notes: "I scribble a few lines and thoughts occasionally on scraps of paper (mostly the backs of letters soliciting alms for victims of wars, social injustice, obscure but terrible diseases, famine; or unpaid bills and threatening exhortations). I consider them posthumous works as they are not fit to print now and I would be embarrassed to acknowledge them. I have considered using pseudonyms, . . . but there are also risks involved."

Well, now they are indeed posthumous, and I hope they do not embarrass her ghost. It is a great relief to me to salvage at least some of this archive now at last.

Genealogy

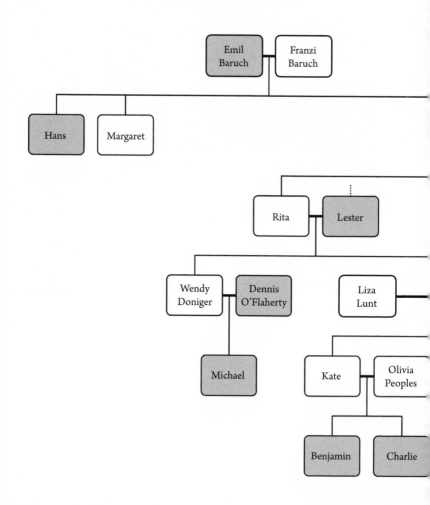

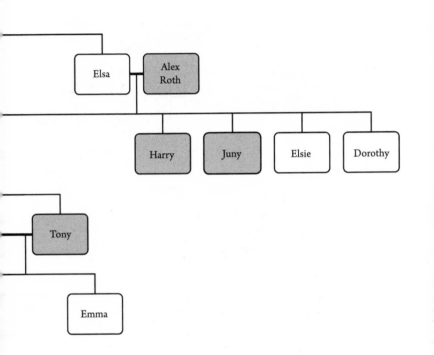

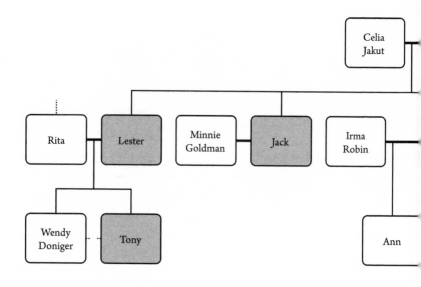

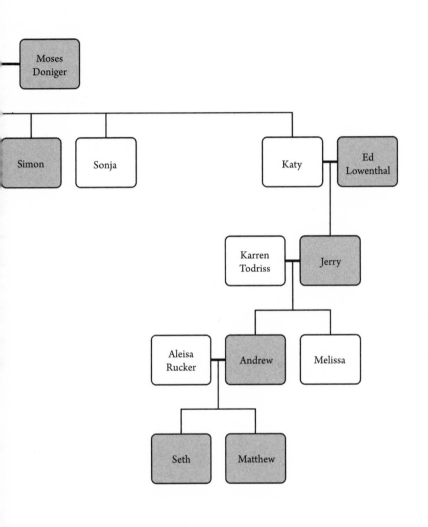

Rita's Notes

Transcribing all of her notes would be a major project, and another book, but I have cited relevant snippets throughout this book, and here are a few more entries to give you a better idea of the range.

To begin with, there are, scattered throughout, a number of one-line, gnomic aphorisms:

Take life from death and what is left?

The trouble with the world is lack of empathy and driving on the left.

I'm over the weather.

The leisure of the theory class.

At times it is difficult to distinguish between aging and maturing.

I have solved the mystery of the missing arms of the Venus of Milo and all other missing limbs, heads, broken noses and all other chips and dents on great works of art: slovenly maids and houseworkers.

The entry on November 12, 1967, is whimsical:

People are always suggesting that we get back to first principals. My first principal was a very mean old spinster who caned reprobate dissenters. Her name was Miss Campbell and I'm glad we don't have to return to her. Let's resort to later principles. They're bound to be more agreeable.

But there are also much longer and much more serious entries, such as this one, dated April 2, 1948:

Can it be true that there is no abstract thought, that it is always the product of its contemporary culture, and the brainwashing of the ruling classes? Is it true that only bad art can come of propaganda art? Can the service of art to politics ever end? Can one tell an artist just to observe and what to say about it? For how long? How does this affect originality? These rules are usually promulgated by inartistic people. Is there or has there ever been an artist (writer, etc.) who suggested or supported the role of artists as polemicists? Art is so many things, and so incomprehensible to so many, popular art depends on the support of the lack of artistic education and development of the populus, on ignorance and lack of culture. Avantgarde and new art is unacceptable to the people because it is unrelated to the familiar present, or past sometimes, and requires cultivation and sometimes erudite taste to appreciate. History is replete with examples of great art out of step with its time. In China, it would be denounced, condemned, abolished; when the peasants couldn't understand Swan Lake, mistaking the costumes for underwear, wouldn't it have been wiser to educate the peasants instead of denigrating the ballet to the level of their ignorance? Whose decision is it, antagonistic versus non-antagonistic contradictions? Who defines it? I've learned what brainwashing is. One can recognize the committed party-liners unquestionably. They appear to be incapable of detached, impersonal observation of anything. Their eyes, ears, minds are prejudiced by dogma. They confuse rationalization with reason. Critique der reinen Vernunft is anathema. Personal castigation replaces abstract thought and argument.

One can see clearly here why Rita never joined the Party, though she always remained committed to the ideals of Communism, despite the doubts she expresses here, and frequently elsewhere, about the dogmatic behavior of Communists.

Some time later, there is a short meditation:

What a pleasure to give a toy to a child. It can be old, secondhand, shopworn, as is (a euphemism for shopworn), even incomplete. To him it is a new and glorious thing. It is the new wonder. Where oh where did we lose track of all this joy and start counting and measuring? Why don't we return and begin again to rejoice in IT itself. See and be intrinsic. We are watching space-fiction on our television screen. It is like the Dutch Cleanser girl, a screen on a screen on a screen. A glimpse into the future through what has become the past for some of us but still is the future for others.

And another:

It isn't mice that scare women. It's unexpected animals. I was suddenly dismayed to find the pretty turret shells I was handling were inhabited. Something with feathery bristly horns crawled out of one onto me and gave me quite a start, as they say. Naturally I jumped a little and gave "a little shriek," like the mouse in "Alice." There's nothing so wonderful about men. they simply always *expect* mice, that's all.

An entry from February 25, 1966, is entitled "haiku for our time":

[1]   atom by atom
     the fallout helpless upon us
     down below

[2] infinity calls
     answer somberly but firm
     I'm not ready yet

[3] shelters beckon us
     It is a troglodyte myth
     that we can survive

One haiku, not on the nuclear theme, can be read as a bitter comment on her own life:

[4] scorn the gilded cage
     the sumptuous anchorage.
     decay breeds mute rage.

And one has a title of its own ("Fair Exchange Is No Robbery"):

     The world has broken even.
     Two lovely children
     replace an old couple.

Which could serve as a rather upbeat epigram on all that this book is about.

Rita's Cheesecake

*Recipe from Rita Doniger, transcribed and annotated by
Wendy Doniger*

INGREDIENTS

8" or 9" round spring pan, greased with butter

½ cup Graham cracker crumbs, even better if you put in
some nutmeg, cinnamon, and a VERY little bit of ground cloves.
You can mix the crumbs and spices in the big bowl you're going
to use for the eggs, or if you buy the crackers and grind them
yourself, in the Cuisinart.

3 eggs

1 cup of sugar, and another 4 or 5 TAB for the sour cream
topping

3 8-oz. packets of Philadelphia cream cheese, i.e., 24 ounces.
Other brands are not quite so good. Low fat or low calorie, or
anything of the sort, is disastrous.

2 pints sour cream

A LOT of pure vanilla extract, perhaps even a full 2-oz. bottle

Have all the ingredients at room temperature if possible.

Grease the pan with butter, dump in the cracker crumbs and
shake it around until the bottom and sides are coated.

Dump the 3 eggs into the Cuisinart or blender and beat them
up for a couple of minutes. Dump them out into a biggish bowl,
using a spatula to get out as much as possible, but don't worry if
some is left in. You don't have to wash the Cuisinart.

Into the still slightly eggy Cuisinart put the cream cheese. Beat it up until it is all creamy.

Add the cup of sugar and beat it up for a while longer until it is all mixed in. Once or twice, stop the machine and use the spatula to scrape off the bit that gets stuck on the sides and push it back into the blades.

Now dump back in the eggs and mix it all up for about a half a minute.

Pour it all into the cake pan and put it in the oven at 350.

While the cake is in the oven, in the bowl that had the eggs in it (you don't have to wash it) mix the sour cream, the vanilla and the 6 tablespoons of sugar, or more — keep tasting it, yum yum — and let it warm up a bit.

After about 45 or 50 minutes, test the cake with a toothpick (it should come out clean, and also the cake shouldn't be wiggly any more when you shake it). Sometimes it needs an hour.

After the cake is out, turn the oven way up, to 450 or 500.

Use the spatula to spread the sour cream mixture over the cake. Take care to pour the mixture around the EDGES, NOT THE MIDDLE, of the cake; if you put it all in the middle it sometimes breaks through and pours down inside, which is still quite edible but looks funny.

Stick it back into the now very hot oven for about 3 to 4 minutes, just until the sour cream is set.

Take it out, let it cool, and chill it in the refrigerator overnight. I usually put a big FLAT plate over the top of it and also put it on another plate, as sometimes it leaks a little.

If you're going to take it anywhere, leave it in the spring mold and between the two plates 'til you're ready to serve it.

Serve small portions; it's very rich.

I always think of this as the Manichean cheesecake because two things about it are very good and two are very evil.

Good: It is absolutely delicious and, as you see, quite easy to make, indeed foolproof.

Evil: The ingredients are quite expensive (if you're recommending it to people like graduate students) and it has about 5,000 calories per serving.

NOTES

1 The German is "Kann mich auch an ein Mädel erinnern, . . .
Wo ist die jetzt? Ja, such' dir den Schnee vom vergangenen
Jahr [translating François Villon's *Ou sont les neiges d'antan?*,
for which I have supplied Dante Gabriel Rossetti's famous
translation]. . . . Aber wie kann das wirklich sein, dass ich
die kleine Resi war und dass ich auch einmal die alte Frau
sein werd? Die alte Frau, die alte Marschallin! 'Siest es, da
geht's, die alte Fürstin Resi!' Wie kann dann das geschehen?
Wie macht denn das der liebe Gott? Wo ich doch immer die
gleiche bin."

2 Wendy Doniger, *Asceticism and Eroticism in the Mythology of
Siva* (Oxford: Oxford University Press, 1973); *Other Peoples'
Myths: The Cave of Echoes* (Chicago: University of Chicago
Press, 1988); *The Ring of Truth, and Other Myths of Sex and
Jewelry* (New York: Oxford University Press, 2017), and so on.

3 There is a brilliant example of a misremembered story about
misremembering on page 8 in Nicholas Delbanco's *What
Remains* (New York: Warner Books, 2000), a book about a
Jewish family very like my mother's.

4 Oliver Sacks, "The Fallibility of Memory," in *The River of
Consciousness* (New York: Alfred Knopf, 2017), 121.

5 Ian Parker, "Profiles: Inheritance: How Edward St. Aubyn
Made Literature Out of a Poisoned Legacy," *New Yorker*,
June 2, 2014: 51–52.

6 Half a century later, I found this story told about the Hindu
god Krishna, who stole the clothes of the cowherd girls
while they bathed in the river. See my *Hindu Myths*, 228–31.

7   Only four of the siblings remained in America: Sonja had
    gone to Brooklyn with the others but then went back to
    Europe, to Sweden, where her sweetheart from Raczki, Issy
    Austern, had emigrated with his family. He had threatened to
    kill himself if she did not come back to him, and her father,
    Moses Doniger, had forced her to marry him, declaring that
    he would not have Issy's blood on his hands. Sonja lived in
    Linkoping all her life. I am indebted to Liza Lunt, Tony's
    wife and chief archivist of the Doniger family, for this,
    perhaps somewhat mythologized, part of the family story.

8   *New York Times*, May 15, 1926. The article noted that
    representatives from six high schools in New York and
    Brooklyn competed in the final oratorical contest.

9   "Oratorical Winner to Enter NYU," *New York Times*,
    September 12, 1926.

10 *New York Times*, April 17, 1931.

11 See www.hotelpolonia.cz/en/, August 23, 2015. The
    Viennese architect Arnold Heynemann did the renovations.
    Previously it had been called the Steinberg Hotel. During a
    reconstruction completed in 1971, it was connected to the
    adjacent houses.

12 By a weird coincidence, Jack's wife, née Minnie Goldman,
    had a brother who was the father of Robert P. Goldman, a
    man whose academic career was agonizingly close to my
    own: Bob Goldman is, like me, a Sanskritist who studies the
    two great Sanskrit epics and sometimes cites Freud. Yet we
    never met until I taught, for three awkward years (1975–78),
    in Bob's bailiwick at Berkeley, where he still teaches today.

13 Congressional Record 113 (1967): 664; Congressional
    Record (1967) 115: 255. See also October 22, 1969.

14 Wendy Doniger, *The Bedtrick: Tales of Sex and Masquerade* (Chicago: University of Chicago Press, 2000) included stories about Tamar and Judah, Rachel and Leah, and Ruth and Naomi.

15 *Pastoral Psychology* 60 (January 6, 1956): 80–81; also cited in Paul Bishop, *Jung's Answer to Job: A Commentary* (London: Routledge, 2002), 19. The Pastoral Psychology Book Club, in Great Neck, also published a new edition of *Answer to Job* in 1956.

16 In a book published in 1987, *Homiletic: Moves and Structures*, David G. Buttrick (iv) acknowledges that Chapters 7 and 9, "Cast and Plot," appeared originally in *Pulpit Digest* LXI (January/February 1981): 53–56; and Chapter 10, "A Fool Farmer and the Grace of God," appeared originally in *Pulpit Digest* LXHI (November/December 1983).

17 Franz Liszt, *Liebesträume No. 3*. The poem is "O Lieb."

> O lieb, o lieb so lang du lieben kannst, so lang du lieben magst.
> Die Stunde kommt, wo du an Gräbern stehst und klagst.
> Und sorge daß dein Herze glüht, und Liebe hegt und Liebe trägt,
> So lang ihm noch ein ander Herz in Liebe warm entgegenschlägt.
> Und wer dir seine Brust erschließt, o tu ihm was du kannst zu lieb,
> Und mach ihm jede Stunde froh, und mach ihm keine Stunde trüb!
> Und hüte deine Zunge wohl: bald ist ein hartes Wort entflohn.
> O Gott — es war nicht bös gemeint — Der andre aber geht und weint.

18   Bing had at first announced that the performance *would* continue, and had summoned the understudy. But then a doctor from the audience had tended to Warren and realized that he had suffered a cerebral hemorrhage. A priest (the secretary to Cardinal Spellman) who happened to be in the audience administered the last rites to Warren, in the presence of his Catholic wife. (Warren, born Jewish, had converted when he married her.) Then Warren died.

Only then did Bing make the final announcement.

19   See Judith S. Goldstein's very informative *Inventing Great Neck: Jewish Identity and the American Dream* (New Brunswick, NJ: Rutgers University Press, 2006), and Jay Cantor's rather disappointing novel *Great Neck* (New York: Alfred Knopf, 2003).

20   Martin Brown's play "The Idol" opened in Great Neck in 1929, but never made it to New York.

21   Great Neck High School actually also produced a third well-known Sanskritist, Kenneth Langer, who, like me, studied with the great Daniel H. H. Ingalls at Harvard. But Langer was in the class of 1968, ten years after Barbara Stoler and I graduated in 1958.

22   Faith Dane was the stripper who, as the character Miss Mazeppa, played a trumpet in *Gypsy* (both on Broadway and in the film) and sang "You Gotta Have a Gimmick." She is also famous for having insisted, successfully, that she had a copyright on that act, which led to a "Faith Dane" clause inserted in theatrical contracts. In her later years, she became a perennial political candidate on the Green Party ticket in Washington, DC.

23 The book was *The Hindus: An Alternative History* (New York: Penguin, 2009; Delhi: Penguin, 2010). See Wendy Doniger, "Banned in Bangalore," op-ed, *New York Times*, March 5, 2014; "India: Censorship by the Batra Brigade," *New York Review of Books*, May 8, 2014.

24 Email from Ramesh B., February 17, 2014.

25 See Arvind Kumar, "The Religious Crusades of the CIA," indiafacts, January 21, 2015, http://indiafacts.org/religious -crusades-cia. Kumar has continued to attack me in dozens of widely posted emails, though without involving my father or uncle. On September 16, 2017, he sent and copied to the entire faculty of the Divinity School, plus the president and provost of the University of Chicago, an email accusing me (wrongly) of being the teacher of several scholars who had displeased him. And on December 7, Kumar sent another email, this one also citing my "relationship with the sex pervert Mircea Eliade" and stating that my "ex-husband who wrote the script for Teenage Mutant Ninja Turtles [this is true; he did] is another suspected CIA agent and worked in Hollywood which has been exposed as a place for sex perverts." Two more men to darken my name.

26 Robert Benchley, "How to Get Things Done," in *Chips Off the Old Benchley* (New York: Harper, 1949).

27 Eventually, the School of Oriental and African Studies subsidized the book (*Asceticism and Eroticism in the Mythology of Siva*, 1973); Oxford University Press published it, and it became a great success, but I didn't know any of that in time to prevent my breakdown. SOAS collected the royalties on the book until, years later, they wrote to me

saying that their subsidy had been repaid, and from then on I got the royalties on the book (renamed *Siva: The Erotic Ascetic* for the paperback), which is still in print.

28   It was my 1973 Oxford D Phil dissertation, *The Origins of Heresy in Hindu Mythology*, subsequently published as *The Origins of Evil in Hindu Mythology* (Berkeley: University of California Press, 1976).

29   Woody Allen, "Fabulous Tales and Mythical Beasts," in *Without Feathers* (New York: Random House, 1976). I've cited this useful beast in several books, most recently in *The Ring of Truth: And Other Myths of Sex and Jewelry* (New York: Oxford University Press, 2017).

30   Some of my limericks were published in a *Festschrift* ("Limericks on the Study of Religion," in *The Incarnate Imagination: Essays in Theology, the Arts and Social Sciences in Honor of Andrew Greeley*, ed. Ingrid H. Shafer [Bowling Green, OH: Bowling Green State University Popular Press, 1988], 298–301); and others, about India, in my collection *On Hinduism* (Delhi: Aleph, 2013).